CONTENTS

Introduction

What did you dream last night? It may have been illuminating or confounding, captivating or relatively uninspiring. Perhaps it was a joyous adventure like none other, or a scene so upsetting it rattled you to the core. It may have included people, places, and events that were all too familiar, or those that were seemingly bizarre and unrecognizable. Likely, it defied your ordinary perception of how space and time operate, leaving you wondering just from where this symphony of mesmerizing visions emerged. Assuming, that is, if you remembered your dreams. On par with the mystery that surrounds what they mean and where they come from is the question of where they go and why they seem to dissolve so quickly. Owing to their evanescent quality, some people even believe that they don't have them at all. However, we all dream.

Dreams gift us with a wide range of rewards. They can shine a light into the inner recesses of our mind so that we can further understand oft-shrouded desires, motivations, and potentials. They offer us insights that can augment our holistic health. They can be powerful tools for enhancing creativity and amplifying our problem-solving abilities, while also helping us tap into a broader universal understanding.

How to Use This Book

I have written *The Complete Book of Dreams* to help you access these rewards and elevate your well-being. I hope that this book inspires your connection to your dream life so that you can live the life of which you've always dreamed. As you will discover, it is both a reference and a guidebook. In it, you'll find troves of information that will further forge your understanding of and appreciation for the power of dreams. Plus, the book includes a wealth of simple exercises and other practical how-tos designed to take your dreaming to the next level. It is organized into three parts:

Part I: Sleep
Since to dream well you need to sleep well, in this part of the book you'll learn about the importance of slumber and natural ways to get more of it.

THE COMPLETE BOOK OF
DREAMS

A Guide to Unlocking the Meaning and Healing Power of Your Dreams

STEPHANIE GAILING

WELLFLEET
PRESS

Part II: Dreams

These chapters feature an exploration of the dreaming mind and a survey of the wide range of dreams that we may have.

Part III: Dreamwork Practices

In this section, you'll learn an array of strategies to remember your dreams, as well as document and decode them so that you can tap into their powerful potential.

The Complete Book of Dreams can be read in numerous ways. One approach is to read it cover to cover, moving through it as it progresses from insights on sleep to an exploration of dreams. Or, you can dive right into any chapter without having to read another; so, for example, if you're interested in amplifying your dream recall, or accessing strategies to sleep better, or seeing how astrology and dreams sync together, or any number of distinct topics featured in this book, you can go straight to that chapter and learn more about that realm. Whether you read the book sequentially or one chapter at a time, you'll see that there are many cross-references included throughout which point you to ancillary information featured in another area; therefore, flowing between different parts is a third way you may find yourself reading *The Complete Book of Dreams.*

Collective Dreaming

For eons, communities would honor the power of the dream, not only for individuals but also for the collective. As global concerns continue to shift, we may see group dreaming practices — such as an approach like social dreaming — become more popular as tools that help us uphold the value that oneiric messages carry for society at large. Relatedly, as we continue to face an existential climate crisis, we may find that the practice of earth dreaming, in which we can gain awareness that helps us foster eco-resilience, becomes of further interest to dreamers across the globe.

PART I:

sleep

CHAPTER ONE

CREATING A SLEEP AND DREAM SANCTUARY

Our bedroom is our most personal and private haven, a space in which we relax and let go, enjoying experiences that are nourishing for our body, mind, and soul. It's the room in which we undertake two of the activities that can powerfully promote our well-being: sleeping and dreaming. And it's also the place in our home in which we generally spend the most time: if you sleep 7 to 8 hours each night, you spend about one-third of your life in your bedroom. Treating it as a sanctuary, a place we cherish and revere, can help us sleep and dream even better. And while our attitudes toward our bedroom can go a long way in terms of elevating its sanctity, there are also practical design steps we can take to help us create a more salutary space that promotes relaxation and well-being. In this chapter, you'll learn some design principles that can enhance your bedroom's energy and flow, how to create a dream altar, and the slumber-inspiring importance of environmental factors such as light, temperature, air quality, and sound.

Bedroom Design Principles

We want to design our bedrooms so that they are as beautiful and comfortable as possible. Additionally, we also want them to emanate a sense of ease and inspire relaxation. To help toward this aim, we can turn to feng shui, the ancient Chinese art of furniture placement and design that is popular today. It offers valuable tips on how to arrange furnishings to allow for energy to more effortlessly flow and peacefulness to feel as if it's streaming throughout. According to feng shui, the bedroom is the most important room in the house, so arranging

7

Seven Sleep and Dream Sanctuary Guidelines

1   Think of your bed as a place dedicated to enjoying some of life's most intimate and soul-enriching experiences: sleeping, dreaming, and lovemaking.

2   Treat your bedroom as a comforting haven where you can find peace and solace.

3   Design your bedroom so it helps you to naturally unwind when you spend time there.

4   Don't bring work — nor other things that activate or agitate your mind — into the bedroom.

5   If you need to have a stirring conversation with your partner or child, opt to do it in another room.

6   Make your bed each morning. Having a tidy and fresh bed into which you can climb each night helps to further invite in restful sleep.

7   If possible, have your bedroom be a tech-free zone, keeping computers, tablets, and even the television in another room.

it thoughtfully is of great value. Here are some feng shui design principles that can infuse your bedroom with more of a sanctuary feel:

■   Remove anything that isn't meaningful and doesn't promote ease and relaxation. The letter from your ex that's stored in your nightstand drawer? That old, frayed, beaten-up chair? The plant that's on its last leg? Move them to another room if you don't want to remove them altogether.

■   Avoid mirrors within the sightline of the bed; as they reflect light, mirrors are thought to amplify the energy in the room, which may interfere with the calming feel that we want our bedroom to have.

■   Be thoughtful about the artwork you choose, having it be of images that represent what you want to manifest in your life.

■   If the ceiling has overhead beams, avoid having furniture such as chairs or your bed under them, or perhaps cover the beams with draping.

- If possible, don't have a bookshelf in the bedroom, since it enhances the active energy of the room. If, owing to space constraints, you do need to have one in there, arrange the books horizontally rather than vertically, to avoid the room's energy feeling as if it's being spliced.

- According to feng shui, neutral and light tranquil colors are better for bedrooms than bright or deep colors like red, orange, purple, and black.

- While it may be ideal to not have a television in your bedroom, if you do have one, position a screen that blocks it from sight when you're sleeping. Or put it in an armoire with a door.

- As best as possible, hide all electrical cords.

- If you need to have gym or office equipment in your bedroom, cover it with a beautiful piece of fabric or obscure it with a screen when it's not in use.

The Bedroom Throughout History

Like most everything, the bedroom has taken on evolving roles depending upon the current culture's needs. It's only been relatively recently that bedrooms have become the private enclaves that they now are. Previously, many families slept in a common room, not only out of economic need but also as a way to foster a sense of community and protect from possible middle-of-the-night intruders. Bedrooms were also public stages where the affairs of life were conducted. It was in this room that many of life's significant activities would take place: weddings, socializing, business deals, births, and deaths. Beds were prized items; rather expensive — even more so than by today's standards — they were status symbols, passed down from generation to generation, and often items included in wills. Today, bedrooms have evolved to reflect the current cultural context and the needs of their denizens. They may serve as playrooms for kids, hideaways and study spaces for teenagers, offices for gig worker...and ideally, a place where we all open to the rejuvenation that comes with our sleep and dreams.

THE BED

Owing to the bed being the centerpiece of the bedroom and the important role it has, feng shui offers numerous principles related to its optimal positioning. It's suggested that the bed should be located in what's known as the "commanding position." In this placement, the bed would be facing the door so that you could readily see it and anyone who enters or exits the room. However, you don't necessarily want it to be exactly in line with the door, as you want to avoid having your feet pointing directly toward it. The head of the bed should ideally be against a solid wall. If the wall behind you has a window, try to alleviate any potential drafts, and also be sure to draw the curtains at night. It's thought best to not hang art over the bed. And try to also avoid placing the head of your bed in a position that has it sharing a wall with the bathroom, notably the one on which the toilet is located. (And speaking of your bathroom, ideally, you shouldn't be able to see it from the bed; if that's unavoidable, remember to keep the door shut.) Solid headboards are thought to provide more stability than those that have slats. The headboard should be positioned so that it's stable and doesn't wobble. You should ideally have space on three sides of the bed, so that there's easy ingress into and out of it. It's not only a practical idea, but one thought to promote more optimal energy circulation.

THE MATTRESS

As we spend about one-third of our life in bed, it makes sense to prioritize having a good mattress. And while it can be a high-ticket item, if we think about how elemental sleep and dreams are to well-being, we can readily see how a good-quality mattress may be the piece of furniture that provides us with the best ROI. One of the premier roles that a good mattress has is to support the alignment of your spine. Not only will this have you be more comfortable and therefore sleep better, but it will also allow you to feel better during the day. It should encourage your spine to maintain a neutral position, with your lower back able to preserve its natural curve. As a general rule, mattresses last five to ten years. It's good to replace yours when it feels lumpy, you start waking up sore, or when you notice that you regularly feel better when sleeping elsewhere. That said, discomfort caused by sleeping isn't solely the realm of our mattress; if you wake up with neck or shoulder pain, it could be your pillow that's the culprit.

NIGHTSTANDS

Nightstands play an important role in the sleep and dream sanctuary. After all, they serve as an accessible resting spot for the items that give us comfort as we fall asleep and awaken — whether that's a glass of water, reading material, an alarm clock, or the like. Plus, their role in assisting us in our dreamwork is highly valuable. They are where we place the tools — such as paper and a writing instrument, or a recording device — through which we document our dream memories. From a feng shui perspective, like everything else in the bedroom, your nightstand should be orderly and clutter-free. If yours is overflowing with stuff, consider whether some of what you're keeping there can be stored elsewhere. Can your supplement bottles be kept in the bathroom? Can all but the current novel you're reading remain on a bookshelf? Can your ambient noise–reducing

Choosing the Best Mattress and Pillow

We've come a long way since the original mattress, which dates back to 77,000 years ago and was composed of reeds covered by insect-repelling leaves. Technological advances have made it so that there are a host of different options — including inner spring, memory foam, hybrid, air-filled, and futons — from which to choose. Which one is best for you depends upon several factors, including your go-to sleep position, whether you run hot or cold at night, if you occupy the bed alone or with someone else, and, of course, your budget.

Also, don't forget about the value of having quality pillows; they play an essential role in promoting well-being by supporting your neck and helping your spine maintain a neutral position, warding off aches and pains that may otherwise occur. Pillow-purchasing considerations include: (1) its loft supports your sleeping style (stomach, side, or back); (2) whether you prefer it is made of natural or synthetic materials; (3) making sure you're not allergic to what it's filled with; and, (4) the price.

machine be placed on a bureau instead? If you do find that you need access to a variety of sundry items, arrange them thoughtfully on a beautiful tray or in decorative boxes, or get a nightstand that comes with drawers. Even if you sleep alone, feng shui principles still recommend that, space permitting, there be a nightstand on each side of the bed, since it will make the area feel more even and balanced. Nightstands with smoother, rather than sharp, edges are preferred.

CLEAR THE CLUTTER

From a feng shui perspective, clutter is not only messy, but it also represents unfinished business that may energetically drain us. It impedes vitality and restricts life from flowing forward. The first rule of bedroom decluttering is to take the things that you've stored under your bed and find a new spot for them. That's because we want the foundation upon which we sleep to be free-flowing, and not the storehouse for things such as books, shoes, or any non-treasured items we don't otherwise know where to keep. If limited space makes it a necessity to use the under-bed area for storage, dedicate it to keeping things that are softer and more neutral (like t-shirts, extra blankets, pillows, etc.). If your closet is in your bedroom, make sure it's in good order. Do a deep cleaning and keep it organized. And regardless of its state of order, keep the door to it closed when you're not using it. The same goes for cabinet drawers. Recently said goodbye to a lover with whom you shared the bed? Do a room clearing by burning sage or palo santo as a way to release their energy. Also, remove any of the things of theirs that you truly don't want around you anymore.

Creating a Dream Altar

Another way that you can transform your bedroom into a sanctuary is to create a dream altar, which can bring more intentionality to your oneiric practice. By doing so, you're creating a dedicated space that reminds you of the power of your dreams and your commitment to seeking the insights they provide. To do so, first find a place that works best for you, whether on a low table, a shelf, the top of your armoire, or even your nightstand. Have it feature items that have personal meaning and significance. To get you started thinking about designing yours, here are some ideas on what it can feature:

- Candles
- Flowers, whether fresh or dried
- Found objects like shells or sea glass
- Small pieces of art
- Photographs of meaningful places
- Pictures of spiritual teachers

- Iconographic figurines
- Tarot or angel cards
- Crystals
- Sacred texts
- Notes that reflect dream intentions
- Palo santo, sage, or incense for smudging

13

Dream Altar Tips

- If you're practicing dream incubation and you want a spot to place a reminder of what creative problem you're trying to solve, you can also make space for it on your altar.

- To heighten the intentionality of your dream altar, remember to do a clearing before you set it up and any time you feel it could use some energetic amplification. You can do this by using palo santo, sage, or your favorite incense.

- When you're traveling, bring along some sacred items, so that you can create a dream altar wherever you are.

- If you share your bedroom with a partner, you can each have your own altar. Or create one together.

- See if your children are interested in having a dream altar in their room. While this may be something more aligned with older kids, it could also be an empowering strategy to help little ones who are struggling with nightmares, as they can put items on it that help them feel safe and protected.

Environmental Considerations

It's not just furniture that has an important function when it comes to our bedroom being a haven for a restful night's sleep. Paying attention to environmental factors such as light, temperature, air quality, and sound may also do wonders.

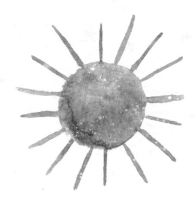

LIGHT

One of the keys to sleeping well and feeling refreshed during the day is modulating the light to which we are exposed. Much of the reason has to do with melatonin. This hormone plays an important role in regulating our circadian rhythms. Its release occurs with darkness, while light suppresses its production. Melatonin is one of the chemical signals in our brains that inspires the sleep cycle. And so, if we want our brains to shift into their somnolent state, having adequate amounts of melatonin is key.

As it turns out, blue light can disrupt sleep cycles, since it tells your body to stop producing melatonin. Therefore, be selective in the lights you use in your bedroom, avoiding certain LED and other bulbs known to feature it. Consider having your bedroom lights be on dimmers so that you can prevent them from being too bright before you go to sleep. Opt for lamps that shine light toward the ceiling rather than downward, as this, too, can create a more relaxed atmosphere. Other sources of blue light are the electrical devices we so readily rely upon in our modern lives. Therefore, avoid using your phone, tablet, and computer close to bedtime. If you can't readily do so, and need to use your tech devices while in bed, get some glasses that block the blue light, or use software programs that will modulate the spectrum of light that your gadgets emit.

If light streams in from outside, consider getting blackout curtains that will encourage there to be more darkness. If your bedroom just isn't dark enough for you, consider using an eye mask. Eliminate or reduce other sources of light; for example, avoid having a clock that has a bright digital readout. While night-lights may have kept us company when we were little kids, they aren't limited to use only by the young. In fact, they may still be helpful tools, allowing us to avoid turning on jarring brighter lights during middle-of-the-night journeys to the bathroom. Look for ones that have a red- or orange-hued bulb, as these will be less stimulating than those that emit the more blue-green light that's reflective of daytime.

As much as we want our bedrooms to be dark at night, we want them to be light in the morning. This helps inspire a feeling of alertness, while also signaling to our body that it should curb melatonin production. Open the curtains to let light filter in. Consider getting a sunrise alarm, one whose light gets gradually brighter in the morning as your wake-up time arrives. If it makes sense for you, get a smart lighting system that you can program to dim, go off, and then gradually go on at specified times.

TEMPERATURE

Temperature also plays a key role in helping us sleep, with thermoregulation integrally linked to our sleep and wake cycles. Our body temperature varies throughout the day, according to our naturally built-in circadian rhythms; it drops as bedtime approaches, with the lowest point being about 2 hours after we enter slumber. Researchers have found that our core body temperature needs to drop a bit to initiate our drifting off to sleep. As such, since the ambient climate of your bedroom can play a key role in lulling you to sleep, lowering it to a target temperature will help to reduce your basal temperature. It's thought that, for the average person, 65°F (18°C) is a good goal, with children and seniors needing it to be a few degrees warmer. If that temperature sounds cold, remember you can always add another layer of blankets to your bed. You can also keep warm upon arising with slippers and a robe accessible by your bedside.

Alternatively, if 65°F (18°C) sounds like an impossible dream in the summertime, or your bedroom heat retention is its gift in the winter but its curse other times of the year, there are temperature-reduction strategies you can employ. Get a fan to circulate the air, as that can make it appear cooler. Open the windows, if possible. You can also try cooling yourself by placing a cold gel pack in your pillowcase. Or, look for pillows made with more cooling fabrics, as well as specially designed mattress toppers that you can program to different temperatures.

AIR QUALITY

More and more research has shown that the air we breathe has significant impacts upon our health. And while we usually associate air pollution with the outdoors, it turns out that indoor air may actually be more contaminated. And while we may not be able to control the air quality of our workplaces or the commercial spots we frequent, we can do so in our homes. If we were going to choose one spot in which to concentrate our air-quality enhancing efforts, it seems that the bedroom would be a good place to start, given all the time we spend there. You may just find that doing so gives your well-being a boost, noticing that you have less congestion, low-level fatigue, brain fog…and, also, better sleep. Here are some tips to enhance your bedroom's air quality:

- Regularly clean your bedroom, including vacuuming the carpets or mopping the wood floors. Consider using nontoxic cleaners that are either fragrance-free or have scents derived from natural essential oils. This would include the detergent you use to clean your linens.

- Consider making the bedroom a shoe-free zone, so you don't bring in dirt from outside. Have slippers by the bedroom door that you can readily put on.

- Make sure your heating sources have good venting, with ducts that are regularly cleaned.

- Watch for water accumulation, to prevent the growth of mold spores.

- Consider getting an air filter to remove ambient pollutants.

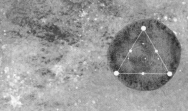

Electromagnetic Fields

Another environmental factor that may possibly have an impact upon our well-being is the presence of electromagnetic fields (EMFs). After all, given that our nervous system and heart operate via electrical signals, some people question whether being constantly surrounded by EMFs, including when we sleep, can have a deleterious effect upon our slumber and our health. At this point, most of the findings that suggest a purported impact of EMFs on health come from anecdotal evidence. The minimal research that has been done hasn't yet drawn a strong correlation. That said, if you feel you are hypersensitive to EMFs, or you just like the idea of fully turning off when your waking mind is turned off, there are some easy things you can do to reduce your exposure to EMFs in your bedroom. Don't sleep near circuit breakers. Shut the Wi-Fi off when you go to bed. Have your alarm clock be battery-operated. And if you keep your phone in your bedroom, switch it to airplane mode.

Indoor Plants

Many plants are thought to act like natural filters, cleaning the air of pollutants such as formaldehyde, benzene, and carbon monoxide; but, while the research supporting this finding isn't yet conclusive, having plants in your bedroom may still be beneficial, as they breathe life into a space, both figuratively as well as literally, since they take in carbon dioxide and release oxygen. Plus, they add natural beauty and may have additional health benefits: research with hospital patients found that plants and flowers placed in their rooms helped reduce anxiety and lower blood pressure. Some of the plants often cited to help with air quality include golden pothos, spider plants, and peace lilies. If you want to infuse some natural fragrances into the room, notably those that are calming, you could consider a jasmine, gardenia, or lavender plant. From a feng shui perspective, corners are a great location for plants, since energy can otherwise stagnate in these spots. Of course, if you have small children or pets, ensure that the plants in which you're interested are not toxic to them. Also, if you have mold allergies, you may need to be more careful about having plants in the bedroom, as the soil may contain spores to which you could be sensitive.

SOUND

Some people can sleep through anything, while others awaken to a drop of a pin. If you're sound-sensitive, you want to do what you can to minimize any auditory interruptions that can disrupt your Zzzs. In addition to reducing background noise, there are also active measures you can adopt to help block your exposure to sounds. For some, earplugs readily do the trick. They come in a variety of shapes and materials — for example, silicone ones mold to your ears, while foam ones are pre-shaped. If you're into tech gadgets, you may want to look into noise-canceling headsets or earbuds. Another option to consider is getting a sleep sound machine. These play white noise or pink noise, the latter of which some people find to be more soothing, as it contains less high-frequency sounds. If you're someone who likes to fall asleep to calming music, program it so that it shuts off automatically after a certain point, so that it doesn't stir you to awaken in the middle of the night. Traveling? Ask for a quiet room — away from the elevator, busy streets, and ice machines — when making your reservation. Also, some hotels feature quiet zones or quiet rooms, so consider this as another quality to look for when researching for your travels.

PART II:

dreams

CHAPTER TWO

THE ARRAY OF DREAMS

Throughout history, scholars who studied dreams have created classification systems to represent the different types that they witnessed. Reviewing these is fascinating, as it clearly reflects how our understanding of and relationship to dreams has shifted throughout time and across cultures. For example, the fifth-century scholar Macrobius put forth a five-fold division of dreams in his *Commentary on the Dream of Scipio*. His classification system held sway for quite a while, including throughout the subsequent medieval period. It included three types of predictive dreams: visio (prophetic dreams that come true), oraculum (dreams that reveal the future), and somnium (enigmatic dreams that require interpretation to discern their meaning). It also included two types of non-predictive dreams: visum (which feature the visitation of apparitions) and insomnium (nightmares, thought to be catalyzed by either physical or mental stress). Although we currently don't have a formal categorization system that everyone uses, what follows is a general sketch of the types of dreams that many people have, and the way that they are generally classified today. Given the significant role that three of these — nightmares, lucid dreams, and somatic dreams — play in the lives of many individuals, each of these will also be highlighted in more detail in subsequent chapters.

Recurring Dreams

As their name implies, these are ones that feature the same, or a very similar, situation repeating itself across numerous dreams. Recurring dreams may occur in a concentrated time period. Or, for some people, these dreams repeat throughout extended periods of their lives, with some finding themselves having dreams similar to the ones that they had when they were children. Recurring dreams are pretty common, with a majority of adults surveyed reporting that they've had them. Often, but not always, recurring dreams have negative or unpleasant tones or themes. For some people, they may be so upsetting that they are experienced as nightmares that periodically or regularly occur. It would seem that a recurring dream may be a clarion call to something toward which our psyche wants us to pay attention. They may reflect something unresolved that's calling for healing.

That said, there are different schools of thought as to why we may have them. For example, from a Jungian perspective, these dreams may reflect the cast-off parts of ourselves that are trying to gain our attention, so that we can integrate them and feel more unified. The Threat Stimulation Theory proposed by neuroscientist Antti Revonsuo suggests that these dreams give us the repeated opportunity to rehearse and refine the ways that we would face and overcome obstacles in waking life. All the while, those who suffer from PTSD may have recurring dreams in which they may continually relive their traumatic experience while they are sleeping.

Telepathic Dreams

Telepathic dreams are similar to precognitive dreams (see next page) in that both are considered to be parapsychological phenomena not able to be currently explained by science. And yet, they differ from each other. A telepathic dream is one in which a person is able to psychically transmit information to another, which then appears in that person's dreams. Sigmund Freud actually gave a nod to the idea in his paper "Dreams and Telepathy," although he supposedly never actually acknowledged belief in the idea. There are numerous anecdotal and clinical accounts of its occurrence. There's also a famous pilot study that took place at a 1971 Grateful Dead concert in Port Chester, New York. Thousands of attendees were invited to "send" thoughts of randomly selected images that were projected on a screen at the concert to a skilled dreamer miles away. Upon awakening, the dreamer reported seeing oneiric images that actually had an impressive correspondence with the art that was mentally projected by the concertgoers.

Telepathic dreams were the focus of ten years of study by esteemed dream researchers Montague Ullman, MD, and Stanley Krippner, PhD, at the Maimonides Medical Center in Brooklyn, New York. Beginning in the early 1960s, they conducted numerous research studies, eventually publishing seven articles in medical journals. While some of their

Been There, Done That...Dreamed That

Related to precognitive dreams may be the experience known as déjà rêvé, that feeling that you've already experienced something, only to realize that you did so in a dream. Some psychologists believe that déjà rêvé may explain déjà vu, that feeling that you've already lived through a current situation: you haven't necessarily been there before in waking life, but have so in a dream.

participants did exhibit these paranormal dreams, given that — as they noted — it's hard to determine such a phenomenon through the scientific method, their findings weren't fully conclusive, and were difficult to replicate. One of the interesting discoveries that emerged from their research was the existence of an environmental variable that seemed to affect outcomes; telepathic dreams were found to be more frequent at times when there was less sunspot activity and fewer electrical storms.

Precognitive Dreams

This is the type of dream in which you envision an event that has yet to occur, but which eventually does so in the future. It focuses upon a happening that you had no other way of knowing about, except through your oneiric visions. Some people consider themselves to be able to foretell the future in their dreams, while others may not consider their dreams to be precognitive until after an event they dreamed about manifests. Precognitive dreams may be more commonplace than many would believe. Surveys have suggested that about half of the general public reports that they've had at least one.

Some argue against the possibility of being able to see the future, whether in waking life or dreams. They note that perhaps it's just probability and coincidence. Yet, others — notably those who have had them, and those who believe in an understanding of time informed by quantum theory — swear them to be a valid phenomenon. While a nascent arena, research studies by Ullman and Krippner looked at this realm, finding that some subjects were able to dream of pictures, randomly selected by another research participant, which they had not previously before seen while awake.

While this may sound like a new-age precept, precognitive dreams are a subject that has been considered for millennia. In fact, in *On Prophesying by Dreams*, Aristotle discusses them. He doesn't necessarily support their veracity, offering that they may just be a coincidence, and yet he doesn't fully refute them either. And as we saw earlier, throughout the Middle Ages, people believed that certain dreams — such as those classified as visio or oraculum — contained insights into the future. One of the more famously cited precognitive dreams was had by Abraham Lincoln. In his dream, which the sixteenth U.S. president recounted to his wife and friends, he saw a casket being drawn by a white horse marking an assassination of a president. Thirteen days later, he was shot and killed.

Nightmares

Nightmares are bad dreams, those in which we find ourselves feeling threatened or deeply upset. They may provoke anxiety and fear, and their powerful emotional salience wakes us up. Given that we are often roused while right in the midst of one, it's no wonder that we may remember them, and that they may stay with us throughout the day (and for some people, throughout their whole life). Nightmares generally occur in the early morning hours, when we're spending more time in REM sleep.

Nightmares are most common in preschoolers, with children finding that they experience them less frequently as they enter their preteen years. Teenage girls report having them more frequently than boys their age. In children, the figures that pose a threat usually appear as monsters, ghouls, or animals, while in adults, they often take the form of other people.

It's thought that those who are more sensitive and have thinner personal boundaries have more vivid nightmares. When we are experiencing periods of helplessness in our waking life, nightmares may be more frequent. However, as upsetting as nightmares are, they are completely normal, with most everyone having them. That is, unless they happen frequently enough to cause significant distress, disrupt our sleep, and leave us with a fear of sleeping. If this is the case, they may be classified as a nightmare disorder, for which consulting a doctor may be beneficial as a means of alleviation.

Night Terrors

Night terrors, also known as sleep terrors, are something that many small children experience. By late adolescence, most who have had them seem to outgrow them. That said, some adults who experience traumatic events and have PTSD-informed nightmares may have night terrors. While the name may have you think that they are a type of nightmare, they actually are quite different. They occur in stage 3 SWS deep sleep, usually during the first third to half of the night. This is in contrast to nightmares, which occur during REM sleep, closer to early morning. Night terrors are sometimes accompanied by sleepwalking. No one is yet certain as to why they occur.

It can be very upsetting to experience your child having a night terror. However, rest assured that they are quite normal — estimates have it that about 40 percent of children do so. Night terrors are characterized by the sleeper sitting upright, often screaming or shouting, exhibiting a frightened expression. And while they are animated and appear to be awake, they are actually not. In fact, it's rather difficult to awaken someone from a night terror, given they are in quite a deep sleep. And it's not something that you likely want to do, as many experts suggest it's better to let a person sleep through it. Most people will have little memory of it happening the following morning. If night terrors are a challenging issue for your child, one strategy suggests waking them up a half-hour before they usually happen, so as to try to avoid their occurrence. Of course, if it's something that's of concern, speak to their pediatrician.

Lucid Dreams

One of the key features of a dream is that we're not actually aware that we're dreaming during them. It's only when we awaken that we become cognizant that we moved through a whole world of visions and experiences. Not so with lucid dreams. In these, while you are dreaming, you are conscious that you are actually dreaming. For some, a lucid-dream experience involves being aware you're in a dream, while for others they may also find themselves with the ability to control factors, including the environment, characters, actions, and more. While this may seem like something straight out of a modern sci-fi movie, lucid dreaming has quite ancient roots. Aristotle noted, "When one is asleep, there is something in consciousness which tells us that what presents itself is but a dream." The Greco-Roman physician Galen recommended lucid dreams as a form of therapy.

Lucid dreaming isn't as uncommon as some may think. In fact, a 2016 meta-analysis — a technique which combines data from numerous research studies — found that over 50 percent of people had noted that they had at least one lucid dream in their lifetime. Lucid dreaming is now being used by some in the psychology field to help clients who struggle with nightmares and PTSD, as well as to inspire greater creativity.

Somatic Dreams

Throughout history, one of the types of dreams that was accorded with a lot of attention were those we've come to call somatic dreams. These are dreams in which we may gather awareness into the condition of our physical body, as well as connect to healing insights. Given that the prevailing paradigm of medicine doesn't emphasize a connection between the body and mind, somatic dreams are not something that currently garners the attention that they did in the past. Still, throughout history, and in cultures throughout the world, turning to one's dreams for both diagnostic and therapeutic messages was quite common. It's not only a type of dream that people recognized, but one that physicians honored and encouraged; in some societies — like that of the ancient Greco-Roman civilization — their value was so heralded that they created sanctuaries where people would go to have healing sleep and dreams.

Perhaps you've had somatic dreams. These are the ones in which you realize that your dreams are carrying forth messages that either point you toward understanding the source of dis-ease in your body and/or curative approaches that you can take to enhance your well-being. Additionally, sometimes somatic dreams leave us with strong sensations in our physical bodies, perhaps as a means of drawing attention to certain areas to which we should pay attention.

Big Dreams

Sometimes our dreams feel mundane, whereas other times they feel quite interesting and fascinating. And sometimes they exceed even that; they are highly memorable, often experienced as if they contained some very significant information or powerful lessons that we, or perhaps others, need to heed. These are what are referred to as "big dreams," a term coined by Carl Jung. Big dreams are the ones that also stick with us and we can't shake. They are the ones that feature heightened visual imagery that becomes etched into our memory. They are the ones that may immediately come to mind when someone asks you about any important dreams you've had in your life. They are the ones that may be remembered as being filled with powerful archetypes, experienced as if they are really tapping us into the collective unconscious.

Big dreams may be upsetting ones, experienced as nightmares. Or they may be joyous and revelatory ones. Cultures throughout time speak of big dreams, those that have shifted the course of people, groups, and history. Some believe that big dreams extend beyond those that have personal significance to us as individuals, to those that are envoys of insights and wisdom for the community. They connect us to something bigger, and have us feel as if we're a part of something larger than just ourselves.

Hypnagogia and Hypnopompia

You know those flashes of imagery that burst forth in your mind's eye when you're lying in bed ready to go to sleep? They have a name. Known as hypnagogia (from the Greek *hypnos* for "sleep" and *agogeus* for "leader"), these dreamlike visions, which occur in that liminal state as you drift off to slumber, often feel somewhat hallucinatory. Different than in regular dreams, in which we may find ourselves actively playing a role, in hypnagogia, we have a sense that we are more like observers than participants. Hypnagogic images tend to flicker and have a kaleidoscopic quality, and the sequence of their appearance seems to lack structural coherence.

While they may feel trippy, they are quite normal and experienced by a majority of people. (That said, if they cause you anxiety, talk to a health-care practitioner.) As striking as they are, we often can't remember them upon awakening, and only recall them if we interrupt them while they are occurring to write them down. One of the most famous proponents of hypnagogia was Salvador Dalí, who used these visions for artistic inspiration. Calling his technique "slumber with a key," he would sit in a chair with a key nestled in his closed palm and allow himself to nod off to sleep. When he did, and his muscles relaxed, the key would drop upon a plate he placed below his hand. The resulting clanging noise would wake him up, upon which time he reflected back upon the hypnagogic images that he just had, and used them as creative fodder.

Akin to hypnagogia is a phenomenon known as hypnopompia. Rather than occur between waking and sleeping, the hypnopompic state occurs between sleeping and waking. Like in hypnagogia, one may have visions that seem strange and extraordinary (hence why they are often referred to as "hallucinations"). It is sometimes accompanied by sleep paralysis, wherein you may perceive you are awake and yet your body is unable to move. Hypnopompic states seem to be less frequently experienced than hypnagogic ones.

CHAPTER THREE

NIGHTMARES

While they are a type of dream, owing to the upset that they invoke, nightmares are anything but dreamy. And, unfortunately, they are anything but uncommon. It's thought that upward of 80 percent of people have experienced a nightmare in their lives, with estimates suggesting that about 5 percent experience them weekly. As discomforting as nightmares are, their frequency does bely something that may give you comfort: as unsettling as they may be, they are a totally normal experience. You're in good company if you have bad dreams here and there; there is nothing actually wrong with having them, besides the obvious upset that they cause.

That said, for some people, nightmares occur so regularly and with such intensity that they impinge upon their quality of life, as well as their ability to consistently get adequate sleep. In this case, one may be experiencing what's known as nightmare disorder (also referred to as anxiety dream disorder), a condition codified in the psychological guidebook, the *Diagnostic and Statistical Manual of Mental Disorders (DSM-5)*. It's estimated that about 4 percent of adults, and a greater number of children, have such powerful recurrent nightmares as to have a significant negative impact upon their well-being (whether because of ensuing emotional upset or fear of sleep). Nightmare disorder could arise in conjunction with post-traumatic stress disorder (PTSD), anxiety, depression, or other psychological conditions, or could be an outcome of an acute period of stress. Those who suffer from nightmare disorder are encouraged to seek professional assistance.

One only has to think about our everyday language to further appreciate how nightmares are an experience to which we can all relate. After all, the definition for the word is not limited to upsetting dreams — rather, it's also used to describe things that occur in our waking life. Whether employed as a noun or an adjective, the term *nightmare* describes situations or people that pose an unpleasant prospect, are difficult to deal with, or bring us fright.

Defining Nightmares

What, actually, is a nightmare? Well, if you ask medical researchers, you'll mostly find some overlap in description, but not necessarily full agreement on the nuances of how to categorically define these events. This could be the reason that among the many studies done to understand their prevalence and etiology, inconsistencies remain. Researchers aside, though, there is a general agreement that nightmares are dreams that are so upsetting and frightening that they wake us up out of sleep. Our nightmares may be filled with situations that we perceive to threaten our very survival, whether that's physically or psychologically; in our dream, we may find ourselves experiencing an assault on our physical security or our self-esteem. Sometimes they are so disconcerting that we can't seem to shake them, with their residue wafting into all corners of our waking consciousness. Years or decades later, many people still remember their first childhood nightmare.

However, not every bad dream is a nightmare. Sometimes we have dreams that contain upsetting situations or yield disturbing feelings, but they don't cause the

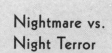

Nightmare vs. Night Terror

Nightmares are quite different than a phenomenon known as night terrors. The former occur during later episodes of REM sleep, wake you up, and are readily remembered. Meanwhile, night terrors occur during NREM sleep, generally within the first 2 hours of sleep onset, and are experienced more frequently by children than adults. In general, we remember our nightmares and yet hardly ever recall the terrifying oneiric subject matter of night terrors when we awaken.

disquietude that a nightmare can. We may have plenty of bad dreams that are striking, but not stirring enough to awaken us; therefore, we recall some of what occurred, but generally not as much as the nightmares that shake us out of sleep. Nightmares, like most other vivid dreams and those with a detailed narrative structure, generally occur during the REM sleep cycle. The length of REM cycles increases as sleep progresses through the night. As such, it seems more common to have a nightmare in the early morning hours rather than soon after you fall asleep.

THE SPIRIT OF THE NIGHTMARE

There are numerous viewpoints on what may inspire nightmares. Before we consider these, though, let's explore a mythic perspective that wove itself throughout numerous cultures, as it can help us to understand not only how people have grappled with nightmares throughout time but also from where the word itself is derived.

Mare is an old English word that denotes a creature that torments or drains the vitality of sleepers. Hence, nightmares reflect the visitation of these evil spirits in the night, during the time of slumber. Mare — also known as *mara, mart, mahrt, moroi,* or *alp* — has appeared in numerous cultural legends, including those of Germany, Croatia, and Russia, as well as Scandinavian and Slavic countries. While each spirit has its own associated myth, in general, a mare would enter into a bedroom in the evening, sit upon a sleeper's chest, and usher in bad dreams.

Legend had it that there were ways to protect against these mythical spirits and the nightmares that they catalyzed. One such strategy included preventing them from entering the room by tightly closing the doors and windows, while also obstructing all the keyholes. To initiate a detour so that they wouldn't find their way to the dreamer, shoes were left by the bedside with their toes facing the door, in the hopes that the mares would reroute themselves through the holes in which the laces were threaded. Other nightmare-prevention action plans included positioning a broom in the bedroom upside down and placing either a bundle of hay or a sharp object in one's bed. Some people would also resort to this more radical mare-dispelling custom: after urinating in a clean bottle and leaving it in the Sun for three days, they would take it to a stream and throw it backward over their head into the water. Customs that seem more aligned to strategies we may employ today to ward off disturbing dreams include sleeping in a different position and saying a prayer.

Why Do We Have Nightmares?

Mares aside, much research and inquiry has focused upon nightmares, investigating how and why they may arise, and how to address them. For some, the etiology of a nightmare may be psychological, while for others, it's a physiological factor that brings them on. What follows are a variety of perspectives on what may underlie the phenomenon.

NIGHTMARES HELP WITH EMOTIONAL PROCESSING

Many feel that through our dreams, we have the opportunity to process daytime experiences and feelings, especially those that we may not have had the inclination to digest and absorb when they occurred. Given that our lives may contain situations that are unsettling, inspire fright, feel threatening, or catalyze a host of other disconcerting emotions, it would make sense that our dreams may sometimes be upsetting, enough so to shake us up and wake us up. Nightmares may also clue us in to the unresolved psychological conflicts that we carry within.

As it turns out, those who are more sensitive, emotionally reactive, and have thinner personal boundaries are more apt to have nightmares. And of course, when we are going through acute periods of situational anxiety, stress, or grief, we may find ourselves having nightmares more frequently as we work through all the feelings in which we are swirling.

Some believe that going through the emotions stirred by an occasional nightmare can be healing, as this may give us an opportunity for processing and expression, rather than avoidance or repression. For those who believe in the prescient potential of dreams, a nightmare could also serve to alert us to an upcoming challenge. And for those who ascribe to the Threat Simulation Theory, a nightmare may be a playscape through which we rehearse actions that we can use in waking life to counter fight-or-flight situations that engender threats to our security.

NIGHTMARES CONNECT US TO THE SHADOW

Nightmares not only wake us up out of sleep, but they can also awaken us to what we may be hiding from our conscious minds. From the perspective of Carl Jung and those who practice Jungian psychology, to understand nightmares — and the route to healing that they may be revealing — we need to understand something called the shadow. The shadow is the part of ourselves that we keep in the dark, the aspects of our personality that we may deem inappropriate, hard to accept, or with which we don't readily identify. It embodies our repressed thoughts and feelings, those that we've disowned, likely due to societal conditioning. Within our shadow may reside emotions that mirror fear, shame, guilt, desire, jealousy, and unworthiness. These feelings may seem so Herculean to carry that we tamp them down and hide them away.

From a Jungian perspective, this then may constitute some of the underpinnings of nightmares: the shadow, crying out to be seen and heard, finds its outlet through dreams. And as it does, it awakens us as it rattles the cage of our emotional equipoise. The dark or gray tone inherent in nightmares reflects the shadow's overtures. In trying to get our attention, it may show up as our being chased, whether by frightening animals, demons, people, or the like. Or it may just appear emblazoned in anything that we find triggering and that blatantly catalyzes fear. And yet, by embracing these shadow elements, we encounter healing and the process of individuation that Jung so prized. Jungians assert that this can allow us to move toward holism, marrying the light and dark aspects of ourselves, weaving all the pieces of our psyche into more of a seamless tapestry. And while this perspective may not necessarily fully take away the sting that we feel when awakening from a nightmare, if we look at disturbing dreams from this orientation, we may be able to more fully appreciate the treasures of insights and healing that they offer.

It's important to remember that there is both a collective, as well as a personal, shadow. Given that some of our dreams seem to connect us directly to expressions of an archetypal nature (those that Jung called big dreams), some of our nightmares may be conduits for understanding what it is that we are together avoiding and collectively disowning. As such, some of our nightmares may be less related to personal issues and more connected to what we perceive society as a whole is repressing, whether that be despair, guilt, disempowerment, or some other form of suffering.

NIGHTMARES AS AN EXPRESSION OF EXPERIENCED TRAUMA

Those who have suffered a traumatic event often experience recurrent nightmares, which involve reminders of the episode from a physical and/or emotional perspective. In fact, having nightmares in which a traumatic event is reexperienced is one of the defining diagnostic criteria for PTSD. About 8 million Americans are estimated to suffer from PTSD, and up to 80 percent of sufferers are thought to experience nightmares. As war is one of the traumatic experiences that can cause PTSD, veterans experience it with more prevalence than the general population. Concurrently, veterans are more likely to have nightmares than the general population; in one well-cited study of Vietnam War veterans, 52 percent of soldiers had nightmares, compared to 3 percent of civilians. Other studies on veterans have found that upward of 90 percent suffer from nightmares.

Traumatic nightmares are different than regular ones, often taking a more violent tone. For some, they involve repetitive dreams that feature an exact reenactment of the anguish-filled event, unfolding as it did exactly — or exceptionally close to — as when it was originally experienced. These dreams may appear like a flashback, with daytime memory seeming to intrude upon the sleeping mind. Some traumatic dreams don't necessarily include the replayed event, but may instead be a canvas for expression of the emotions that were experienced because of it, with symbolic situations expressing terror, fear, and/or survivor guilt. Traumatic dreams are not limited to occurring in REM sleep, like regular nightmares. They may also occur in NREM sleep and be experienced as night terrors. Healing from traumatic events is often reflected in nightmare resolution.

Depression and Nightmares

Not surprisingly, those with depression may have nightmares more frequently. Part of this may be explained by the finding that those with affective disorders oftentimes have challenges sleeping, which can lead to ensuing shifts in sleep architecture that contribute to the greater possibility for nightmares to occur. Not getting adequate sleep can lead to being exhausted during the day, which can impinge upon coping abilities and emotional well-being, which can exacerbate the depression-nightmare-insomnia cycle.

While some who experience PTSD-associated nightmares opt for medication, there are other behavioral approaches that have received widespread attention for their benefit, including Image Rehearsal Therapy. Lucid dreaming may also hold promise in helping people release the hold that traumatic dreams may have.

PHYSIOLOGICAL CAUSES OF NIGHTMARES

For some people, it may be physiological, rather than solely psychological, factors that give rise to their nightmares.

Medications

Certain medications are associated with the more frequent reporting of nightmares. These include antidepressants belonging to the SSRI (selective serotonin-reuptake inhibitor) category, the withdrawal from which has been associated with increased nightmares by some people. Other medications that may have similar effects include certain beta-blockers, high-blood-pressure medications, and L-dopa, the latter which is commonly used for Parkinson's disease. If you have frequent nightmares and just started taking a new medication, talk to your doctor or pharmacist to see whether bad dreams are a side effect of your prescription.

Sleep Patterns

Research studies have noted that those who have insomnia may be more likely to have frequent nightmares. Unfortunately, this can become a self-perpetuating cycle, as nightmares can lead to insomnia, owing to fear of going to sleep. This can cause sleep deprivation, which reduces resiliency and increases stress, which can then lead to more nightmares. In addition to bad dreams being more prevalent in those who don't get adequate sleep, researchers also suggest that long sleepers (those who sleep more than 9 hours a night consistently) also have more nightmares.

Other Causes

Because it shifts sleep architecture, triggering a greater concentration of REM during later cycles of sleep, heightened alcohol use has been found to be associated with nightmare occurrences in some people. Additionally, alcohol withdrawal has been found to have a similar effect. Some people with untreated sleep apnea have been found to more frequently have nightmares; using a continuous positive airway pressure (CPAP) machine may alleviate the recurrence of disturbing dreams. In some studies, stimulants such as caffeine, cocaine, and amphetamines have been found to be associated with higher occurrence of nightmares.

Rescripting the Nightmare: Image Rehearsal Therapy

Image Rehearsal Therapy (IRT) is a behavioral-based approach to treating nightmares that has garnered recognition for its efficacy. Regardless of whether a person's disturbing dreams stem from a traumatic event, are a corollary of PTSD, accompany a psychological condition such as depression or anxiety, or are just an ordinary idiopathic nightmare, IRT may be of benefit. Developed by Barry Krakow, MD, in the 1990s, IRT was recommended by the American Academy of Sleep Medicine (AASM) as a treatment for both nightmare disorder and PTSD-associated nightmares in its 2018 position paper.

IRT is a form of cognitive behavior therapy, a psychosocial orientation that suggests that psychological conditions stem from

Phobetor: God of Nightmares

In Greek mythology, Phobetor was the god of nightmares. With his name meaning "fear," he was the carrier of bad dreams, often appearing as an animal or a monster in oneiric visions. He was one of the sons of Hypnos (the god of sleep) and Pasithea (the goddess of relaxation). Phobetor belonged to the Oneiri, a group of deities who personified dreams, which also included two of his brothers, Morpheus and Phantasos. While Phobetor was the name by which humans knew him, the gods called him Icelos. Many trace the mention of Phobetor to Ovid, in his opus *Metamorphoses*.

Common Nightmares

Numerous studies have been done over the years investigating common nightmare themes. One of the earliest ones dates back to the 1930s, when psychologist Husley Carson questioned over 250 people about the content of their disturbing dreams. Here's an overview of some of the most common nightmare themes uncovered in these studies:

- Physical aggression
- Interpersonal conflicts
- Failure
- Helplessness
- Health concerns
- Death
- Being late
- Falling
- Being chased
- Feeling paralyzed

faulty or unhelpful ways of thinking, as well as learned patterns of unsupportive behaviors. By addressing these thoughts and behaviors, cognitive behavior therapy has yielded promising results in treating a host of conditions. There are two main components to IRT: redefining the relationship between the dreamer and the nightmare, and a reimagining process in which the dream is rewritten.

DREAMER-NIGHTMARE RELATIONSHIP

This stage involves transforming the dreamer's association with the nightmare from one of identity to one of behavior. Instead of seeing themselves as a nightmare sufferer, they revise their perspective to see themselves as a person who has nightmares. The difference is not just semantic: there is a sense of empowerment that comes with realizing that having a nightmare is a behavior, which can be recast, rather than an aspect of identity, which is more fixed than mutable.

REIMAGINING THE DREAM

In this stage, what's first emphasized is the power of imagery, recognizing your capacity to invent stories and create new narratives, and your ability to see them visually in your mind's eye. From there, you then follow these steps:

1 Thinking of a recurrent nightmare you have, you imagine a new story arc that it can take that doesn't include the upsetting or agonizing aspects. You come up with an alternative scenario, rewriting the dream's plot, whether it be the outcome or a feature that you find triggering. Some practitioners have you write out both the original and the reimagined dreams, while others only suggest scribing the new dream, so as to avoid further emphasizing your connection to any traumatic elements in the original one.

2 Throughout the day, you allocate your attention to your reimagined dream.

3 Before bed, you replay the rewritten dream in your mind, telling yourself in a confident and encouraging way that this is the dream that you will have.

Doing the practice requires a minimal time commitment (about 15 to 20 minutes per day). And, as simple as it sounds, IRT is quite powerful. Research and clinical experiences have found that nightmare-reduction benefits may occur within weeks, and even after the practice is discontinued, benefits may still be present. IRT can be done with trained practitioners in an individual- or group-counseling setting. For those who may not want or require professional support, self-help resources like Krakow's *Turning Nightmares into Dreams*

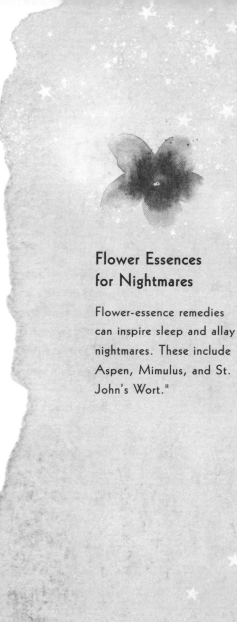

Flower Essences for Nightmares

Flower-essence remedies can inspire sleep and allay nightmares. These include Aspen, Mimulus, and St. John's Wort."

Self-Compassion as Treatment

Researchers have suggested that those who maintain a negative attitude toward themselves may be more inclined to experience nightmares. Given this, showering ourselves with love and forgiveness may offer yet another benefit to our well-being: being a practice that helps us counter having disturbing dreams. Here are some ways to weave more self-compassion into your life:

- Remember that there is no such thing as perfection.

- If something feels challenging, tell yourself that you're doing the best you possibly can.

- Every day, undertake one random act of kindness on someone else's behalf, and one on your own.

- Each evening, write in your journal at least one thing for which you are grateful.

- If you have a tendency to blame yourself for things that aren't even your responsibility, try Pine flower essence.

The Power of Rituals

Rituals give us grounding and have us feel that we can exact action at the behest of an intended outcome. Traditions have held that certain rituals could help to mitigate the impact of bad dreams. In Mesopotamia, they would tell their nightmares to pieces of clay and then throw them in the river to try to dispel the bad dream. The ancient Greeks would share their nightmares with the Sun, believing that its light was a spell-breaker and would cast away the darkness. However, the power of rituals to help counter nightmares may not be solely found in lore of previous times. In fact, recent studies have noted that performing rituals before experiencing a situation anticipated to be stressful can help reduce anxiety. So, if you worry about having a nightmare, doing a pre-sleep ritual may help to calm and center you. This may not only help you to get to sleep more readily, but provide your mind with less anxious fodder that it can translate into a bad dream.

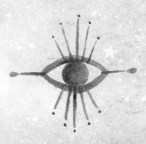

Other Therapies That Take Aim at Nightmare Disorder

In its 2018 position paper, the American Academy of Sleep Medicine shared a variety of treatments that may be beneficial for nightmare disorder. Many of these were behavioral approaches, which is good news for those who want to avoid using pharmaceutical medications. In addition to IRT already discussed, among the other therapies featured were hypnosis, lucid-dreaming therapy, and progressive deep muscle relaxation. Eye movement desensitization and reprocessing (commonly known as EMDR) is also one of the treatments that they gave a nod to when it comes to potentially treating PTSD-associated nightmares.

There are many practices shared throughout the book that can help inspire relaxation, which may have the additional benefit of warding off nightmares.

EXERCISE

The Power of Intention Setting

Another ritual that may help assuage nightmares is doing a modified version of dream incubation. Instead of doing this practice with a particular problem-solving aim in mind, you simply focus your intention on having a pleasant dream. Before going to sleep, give a short and sweet instruction to your psyche, something to the extent of "Dream, please provide me with insights of awareness in a gentle way" or "Dream, please be filled with pleasant experiences." It may seem simple, yet intention setting can be a powerful transformative agent.

CHAPTER FOUR

LUCID DREAMS

A unique feature of dreams is that we generally don't realize that they are occurring until they no longer are. As we dream when we sleep, it seems that we're often asleep during our dreams, needing to awaken to wake up to the recognition of the oneiric journey that we just experienced. But not always. It's possible to have a dream in which while it's occurring, we're able to recognize that we're actually dreaming. We're sleeping, yet not asleep to the fact we're presently dreaming. We become an awakened witness to our oneiric visions, with a cognitive cogency that perceives what is occurring. Realizing that we're in a dream, we may then choose to transform ourselves from a passive character to an active agent who can knowingly traverse dream landscapes and encounters. We can give shape to our experience, whether that means choosing to fly, transform the monsters who haunt our nightmares into allies, work through creative problems without the usual confines of Cartesian limitations, or the like.

This phenomenon is called lucid dreaming. And while for those who have never experienced it, it may sound like a plotline for a sci-fi movie (*Inception*, anyone?), it's actually something that is relatively common. In fact, it's been noted that 55 percent of people have experienced at least one lucid dream in their lifetime, with just shy of one-quarter claiming to have a lucid dream at least once a month. For those who have lucid dreams, it seems that it's an experience that begins spontaneously in adolescence.

Lucid Explorations

Lucid dreaming is considered a hybrid state of consciousness — you're in REM sleep, although not passively dreaming, and yet you're not awake, either. In this space where there's a weaving together of different levels of consciousness, you can be an oneironaut,

Who Experiences Lucid Dreams?

Lucid dreaming has been found to be more commonplace in those who have certain personality traits — such as openness to experience, thin boundaries, and high imaginative function — similar qualities to those who have high dream recall. Additionally, the ability to maintain concentration and exhibit mindfulness may be helpful in lucid dreaming, reflecting studies that have shown that long-term meditators are more likely than non-meditators to be lucid dreamers.

able to explore a host of things that you may not otherwise readily be able to. After all, as you realize that dreams don't have the stability and fixity with which you had associated them, they become a canvas upon which you can more freely be an auteur. Without defenses and presuppositions both about yourself and what reality is, you can deconstruct limiting beliefs and viewpoints. You can fulfill wishes, rehearse behaviors, have adventures, and enjoy heightened sensations. You can practice skills, refine athletic moves, and learn to better understand yourself.

Lucid dreaming can be a source of spiritual understanding, an avenue to further perceive the extended nature of reality. Without your waking life defenses, you may also be more open to seeing and embracing your shadow, the oft-denied facets of ourselves to which we don't readily admit. Some have even noted that they have been able to heal illnesses through being in a lucid-dreaming state. Additionally, it's possible to rescript nightmares, which can lead to their abatement, a possible benefit reflected in the American Academy of Sleep Medicine's 2018 position paper that included lucid dreaming as a potential treatment for nightmare disorder.

THE LUCID-DREAMING BRAIN

How can it be that we're in this liminal state, with an awareness that approaches waking consciousness while we're asleep, being in a dream while knowing we are in a dream? Research and brain-imaging studies may hold some clues. Our brain activity shifts when we are sleeping. One of the hallmarks of a sleeping and dreaming brain is that one of its areas, known as the prefrontal cortex (PFC), is more dormant than when we are awake. As the PFC is responsible for executive function — including rational judgment, self-consciousness, and working memories — usually when we're dreaming, we do so without an editor, judge, or witness, and without self-awareness.

However, when one is lucid dreaming, their brain looks different. EEGs taken during the REM-sleep state of those lucid dreaming show their brains don't behave like they do in normal dreaming. There's more electrical activity happening, reflective of a different level of functioning than usual. This may be why during lucid dreaming people experience metacognition and the subsequent ability to reflect upon their mental state, able to participate in more thought monitoring than during regular dreaming. In addition to knowing that one is dreaming, there's a greater ability to remember episodes of waking life and volitionally control one's actions. While the PFC is more activated than it is during regular REM dreaming, it's still more tamped down than when we are awake. Hence, why lucid dreaming is described as a somewhat hybrid state.

A BRIEF HISTORY

Before we explore techniques that lucid dreamers use to have awareness-filled dreams, let's look to see how our knowledge of conscious dreaming's potentiality has evolved. Lucid dreaming galvanized attention in the 1980s, thanks to the pathfinding work of Stephen LaBerge, PhD. A vanguard in the field, LaBerge focused his post-graduate research in psychophysiology on the subject while studying at Stanford University. This work and his subsequent research endeavors led to his developing a multitude of methods that are still considered foundational for those who follow this practice. Since this time, lucid dreaming has become a focus of study for scientists around the world, with scores of research studies on the subject published in peer-reviewed medical journals.

Conscious Dreaming

While lucid dreaming appears to be a modern-day pursuit, the acknowledgment that states of consciousness are not as demarcated as is often perceived is at the root of many spiritual traditions. These are the ones known for reverentially weaving a tapestry between the waking and dreaming states. Shamanic healers journey in dreams for healing insights. And in Tibetan dream yoga, you explore the nature of mind through maintaining awareness in the dreaming state to be able to experience a wider breadth of spiritual understanding.

However, it was 120 years prior to LaBerge's establishment of the groundbreaking Lucidity Institute that the pioneering tome *Dreams and How to Guide Them* was published. This initially anonymously penned book was later recognized to be authored by the French scholar Marquis D'Hervey de Saint-Denys. The treatise was based upon twenty years of research and examination of lucid dreaming by Saint-Denys, who many regard as the modern-day father of lucid dreaming. The possibility that one may have awareness in a dream was not something that was actually siloed from the psychological field. In fact, Sigmund Freud gave it a nod, noting "there are people who are quite clearly aware during the night that they are asleep and dreaming and who thus seem to possess the faculty of consciously directing their dreams" in a footnote in the 1909 second edition of his classic *The Interpretation of Dreams*. Yet, it wasn't until 1913 that the term *lucid dreaming* itself was forged. The originator of the phrase was Frederick van Eeden, a psychiatrist and the author of *A Study of Dreams*. He defined the experience as not only being able to have an awareness within your dreams, but also one in which "the sleeper remembers day life and his own condition, reaches a state of perfect awareness, and is able to direct his attention, and to attempt different acts of free volition."

Lucid-Dreaming Tools and Techniques

Research suggests that if you have confidence that you'll remember your dreams and you make an intention to do so, you will more likely recall them in the morning. Similar principles seem to apply with lucid dreaming. You can sow the field of conscious-dreaming potential, priming the pump, if you will, by just wanting to do so and telling yourself that it is possible.

From there, lucid dreamers use a variety of different techniques to inspire lucidity in their oneiric journeys. Different people find that certain lucid-dreaming techniques work better for them than others; therefore, experimenting with different ones may help people discover those that best align with them. While providing detailed instruction and guidance about how to lucid dream is outside the scope of this book, what follows are some of the more popular approaches that people use.

MNEMONICALLY INDUCED LUCID DREAM (MILD)

This is one of the classic methods created by LaBerge for inducing lucid dreams. The MILD method can be done when you're first going to sleep or in the middle of the night, coupling it with the Wake Back to Bed technique on the next page.

During the day, choose a dream that you recently had in which you did not experience lucidity. Run through the dream in your mind several times, looking to see if you can find any dream signs that reside within. Once you do, work on rescripting the dream, seeing yourself recognizing these as signals that you were actually dreaming. And then imagine a different path that the dream would take if you had that level of awareness. Reflect on this rescripted dream numerous times daily.

Then, when you're in bed and ready to sleep, create a lucidity affirmation in which you tell yourself that the next time you're in a dream, you will know that you are. This is a bit like dream incubation, where your conscious mind is encouraging your dreaming mind to have a certain level of awareness.

Finally, as you continue to feel lulled to sleep, go back over your rescripted dream, seeing it again and again in your mind's eye. The experience of reflecting upon being lucid, as well as having your mind be playing out a dream in the liminal state before you sink into sleep, helps to prime the psyche to have proximity to the experience of lucidity.

WAKE BACK TO BED

Another practice that lucid dreamers use involves sleep interruption, and is usually referred to as Wake Back to Bed. Given that REM sleep occurs about every 90 minutes for the average person, and the further into sleep we are, the longer the REM periods last, dreamers set their alarm clocks about 5 hours or so after going to sleep. This enhances their chance of waking up in an extended REM period. They then try to stay awake for a while, reflecting upon the dream experiences they just had; for many, doing so helps them slip right back into a lucid-rich REM dream period once they fall back to sleep.

WAKE-INITIATED LUCID DREAMING (WILD)

Hand in hand with Wake Back to Bed is Wake-Initiated Lucid Dreaming (WILD). It's the experience of moving from waking to dreaming with awareness that you're going to shift right into a dream (and, therefore, be having lucidity). As you're doing so, you're reminding yourself to notice such things as hypnagogic imagery, heavy feelings in the body, or other sensations that fill the liminal space between sleeping and dreaming. This is thought to help you slip with awareness right into a lucid dream, all the while reminding yourself that you will remember you are dreaming.

DREAM MASKS

There are numerous masks available that people use to trigger awareness that they are dreaming, an invention pioneered by LaBerge. Worn during sleep, the mask recognizes — through detecting eye movement — when you are in REM sleep. As it does, a light pulses on and off that you can sense through your eyelids. Since you would have previously made the association that the appearance of fluctuating light is a dream sign, it can trigger a moment of lucidity.

GALANTAMINE SUPPLEMENTS

An alkaloid substance known to increase acetylcholine and enhance memory, galantamine in its over-the-counter supplement form is often used for its dream-enhancing properties. (In its prescription form, it's been approved by the U.S. Food and Drug Administration for the treatment of Alzheimer's disease.) As it intensifies REM sleep, it's one of the premier compounds currently used by lucid dreamers to enhance lucidity, with research suggesting that it increases the frequency of these types of oneiric experiences. Before considering using galantamine, check with your health-care practitioner or pharmacist to ensure that it won't have a negative interaction with any current medications that you are taking or health conditions you have.

Staying Lucid

Lucid dreamers have numerous techniques they use to keep themselves in a lucid dream. Given that strong emotions often push us out of sleep, and the experience of being lucid may be quite enthralling, they remind themselves to stay calm and centered while dreaming. Some also encourage themselves to spin their dream bodies, as that seems to postpone awakenings. Another often-used trick is that they instruct their dreaming body to rub their hands together. Focusing upon this sensation is thought to help tune out sensations in the waking world that could help to sway one's dreaming attention.

Looking for Dream Signs

One way to assess whether you are dreaming is to identify what are known as dream signs. These are the signals that indicate you are actually in a dream, as they are events that either likely or definitely cannot occur in waking reality, characteristics that only occur in the dream state.

A good place to start in finding your dream signs is to go through your dream journal, reviewing it to see whether there are places, events, people, or perspectives that forge recurring roles in your dreams. Pay special attention to those that don't appear in your waking life at all or don't appear in the same pattern as they do in your dreams.

Compile a list of these dream signs, perhaps dedicating a page or so in your dream journal to them for handy reference. Before you go to sleep, review these dream signs. This way, you'll be honing your attention so that if you see them in your dream, you will be more likely to recognize that you are actually dreaming.

CHAPTER FIVE

SOMATIC DREAMS

Cultures with healing traditions that honor the connection between the mind and the body perceive that certain dreams offer insights that can help us to understand and improve our well-being. In this chapter, we'll explore these types of oneiric visions, referred to as somatic dreams. We'll do so by discussing the ancient dream temples, as well as the perspectives of physicians and philosophers esteemed throughout history. We'll also look to several systems of traditional medicine in which dreams play an important role in both diagnosis and treatment. In addition, we'll explore the range of expression that somatic dreams can take, as well as recent research that may shine light on what they can reveal, and how we can turn to our dreams for healing insights.

Sanctuaries of Dream Healing

Back in times past, dreams played an integral role in the collective approach to healing for many societies. One of the most stellar examples of this was the prominence in some ancient cultures of sacred dream temples. Think of them somewhat akin to our modern-day medical spas. Those seeking relief from illness would travel to these sanctuaries and engage in prescribed rituals, in hopes of having a dream that would include healing insights.

These sanctuaries include ones found in ancient Egypt that date as far back as four thousand years ago. Many of these dream temples were dedicated to Imhotep, once chancellor to pharaoh Djoser, who was later deified as a god of medicine and healing. As part of a healing regimen offered at these sites, those looking for respite would be lulled to sleep through hypnotic suggestions; these were given by the temple priests and priestesses, who would later interpret the supplicants' dreams. The sleep-lulling prompts were thought to influence a person's ability to connect to divine healing inspiration in their sleep. The Egyptian sleep sanctuaries laid part of the foundation for what currently remains one of the better-known dream sanctuary traditions: the Asklepieia, the ancient Greco-Roman dream temples.

THE ASKLEPIEIA

If you think back to the pantheon of Greek deities, you may remember Asclepius. While many recall him as the god of medicine, what is not as well known is how dreams comprised a large role in the healing system that he forged and practiced. According to Edward Tick in *The Practice of Dream Healing*, Asclepius's father, Apollo, gave his son "prophecy and dream visitations as divine gifts." Physician-priests who followed in the traditions of Asclepius created healing temples throughout the ancient Mediterranean region that were named after him: they were collectively known as Asklepieia, with singular temples called Asclepeion. About three hundred of these ancient temples of dream healing have so far been discovered. The most famous Asclepeion dates back to the fifth century BCE and is located in Epidauros, in the northeastern area of the Peloponnese region of Greece, which is said to be Asclepius's burial site.

Those looking for healing would travel to an Asclepeion. There, they would engage in a series of purification rituals, which included dietary restrictions, ritualistic bathing, and the use of therapeutic herbs. Some of the temples featured large amphitheaters where dramatic productions would take place, meant to inspire the stirring of emotions and resultant cathartic release. This preparatory work was thought to invoke the supplicant's conscious participation in the healing process, including cultivating their faith as well as their psychological readiness.

This was all done in advance of their entering into a special chamber, known as an *abaton*. Here, they would sleep, either on the floor or on stone beds covered with animal pelts. Walking barefoot and dressed in special robes, they would be escorted to the abaton by a physician-priest, who would lead them in a final prayer before they were left in silence to sleep and receive a healing dream. Temple sleep was known as *enkoimisis*.

Once asleep, they awaited the "arrival" of Asclepius or his proxies — snakes, dogs, and roosters — in their dreams. It was said that the dream god sometimes would ask questions and then offer curative suggestions, such as herbs, medicines, foods, or rituals. Other times, spontaneous healing was said to occur through a direct encounter; this could arise from just seeing Asclepius in a dream, or having his surrogate animals appear to touch the dreamer. There are even reports of some people recounting that they were operated upon. Often, Asclepius would invite the dreamer to create art — including composing songs or skits — as a means to further their healing, owing to the perceived ability of these activities in restoring emotional balance.

Still, it wasn't always that the dream's therapeutic value was immediately obvious. It's said that sometimes Asclepius would incorporate riddles or puns into them, which needed to be deciphered. This was one of the reasons that part of the healing ritual included having the physician-priests act as interpreters, helping to discover and discern what came through in a dreamer's nighttime visions, further amplifying the healing.

And while all this may sound extraordinary, there are numerous accounts of people arriving at Asklepieia with physical and emotional maladies, only to leave these sacred healing spots replete with health. These records include not only inscriptions carved into the temple walls but also plaques and votive offerings placed as symbols of gratitude; these votives were often in the shape of body parts, inscribed with the donor's name, presumed to have been the area of healing in which they experienced relief. Reflecting upon these ancient temples gives us a historical and cultural context for the role that dreams played in ancient civilizations. It also shows us the inherent healing power that dreams may have.

Somatic Dreams: A Historical Perspective

When we view the dream temples through our current-day lens, they may seem rather odd. However, if we put them in the context of the times, it makes more sense. In ancient civilizations, part of the reverence accorded to dreams was their healing benefit, which was not just limited to the emotional realm; rather, dreams were also viewed as a means to further understand and bolster physical well-being. After all, for most of history, health was seen as unitive, with the body, mind, and spirit having an integrated relationship. If we see illnesses as having a psychospiritual component, we can further understand how dreams may be valuable in their ability to reveal insights about our physical health. Let's take a look at some esteemed figures in the history of medicine to further frame the context in which dreams were understood.

HIPPOCRATES

Hippocrates, often referred to as the father of Greek medicine, was one of the first to write about dreams and physical health, including in his work *On Dreams*. Many of the medical treatises with which he is associated include reference to the role of sleep and dreams, and the diagnostic value they hold for understanding somatic symptoms. For example, in one of his books he noted that dreams of fountains may indicate a disorder stemming from the bladder.

ARISTOTLE

Aristotle wrote three books on the subject of sleep and dreams: *On Sleep and Dreams, On Sleeping and Waking,* and *On Divination Through Sleep*. He suggested that dreams evolved as a result of sensations we had in our waking life, as well as what our minds perceived occurring in our bodies during sleep. As such, he noted that within dreams, we may be able to find information on events taking place somatically, reflecting the notion that oneiric visions can have diagnostic functions.

GALEN

Galen of Pergamon was a well-regarded physician thought to have forged the foundation of Greco-Roman medicine. The author of *On Diagnosis in Dreams*, he did some of his early medical training at an asklepeian healing temple. One of the principles that he promoted was that dreams have healing and medical diagnostic abilities. He seemed to have believed that physicians had a special capacity to make prognostications related to dreams, noting that these were superior to those made by diviners and others who interpreted oneiric visions.

AVICENNA

Ibn Sina, also known as Avicenna, was a highly regarded physician of the medieval Islamic world whose work influenced medical-school curriculum for centuries to come. He noted how images in dreams may reflect different body constitutions; for example, those with hot temperaments may dream more of the Sun while those with cold temperaments may dream of being submerged in freezing water. He asserted that dreams could also help identify imbalances in humours, the four fluids that formed the centerpiece of medical thought in ancient and medieval medicine.

Types of Somatic Dreams

Even if our current medical approach doesn't feature a consideration of dreams, that's not to say that there aren't people studying this field, nor numerous reports of dreamers who've had firsthand experience with health-related dreams. There are also many anecdotal reports of people who have had somatic dreams related to their physical health. Somatic dreams generally fall into one of four categories, including:

DIAGNOSTIC

These dreams, also called prodromal or pathognomic dreams, occur before either the onset of noticeable disease symptoms or a disease diagnosis. There are numerous accounts of people who have had dreams that contained imagery that had them wondering whether they had a health condition. While they may not have had outward symptoms reflective of a disease, and therefore remained without diagnosis from a physician, they convinced their doctor to perform the necessary tests, only to find confirmation. For some of these people, their dreams were able to save their lives; if left untreated, their illnesses may have led to health deterioration and/or death.

SYMPTOMATIC

These are dreams that a person may have after they realize that they are experiencing dis-ease or have been diagnosed with a health condition. Through these dreams, they may gain more insights into physiological shifts that have taken place in their body. These dreams may also allow for the working through of emotions that have been catalyzed owing to their condition or the impact that their symptoms have upon them.

PRESCRIPTIVE

Like in the dreams of asklepeian supplicants, many people have reported that they received oneiric insights about a pathway to take to resolve a current illness or stem the possibility of the development of one. One famous example of this comes from the account of British architect Sir Christopher Wren. Upon his taking ill, he postponed having a bloodletting treatment until the following day. The dream he had that evening included scenes of palm trees and a woman offering him some date fruits. The next morning he decided to eat some dates and subsequently found himself to be healed of his illness.

CURATIVE

There are also accounts of people being spontaneously healed in their dreams. While the imagery varies, some report that in the dream itself someone appears and says that they will help heal the sufferer and/or performs an act of healing in the dream. They then subsequently find that their symptoms have mitigated upon arising, or shortly thereafter.

EXERCISE

Tuning in to Your Somatic Dreams

Now that you know more about these types of oneiric visions, survey your dreams to see whether you've ever had one (or several) that were somatically informed. For example, thinking back to the last time you weren't feeling well, look back in your dream journal to the dreams you had around that time. See whether there are any symbols that appeared that, in retrospect, seem like they were reflecting the experience of dis-ease. If so, keep note of them in case they appear in subsequent dreams.

You can also use the dream incubation technique to try to discover curative solutions for when you're feeling under the weather. Before going to bed, ask your dreams to reveal insights on dietary guidance and self-care practices that may help you feel better. In the morning, look to what arose in your dreams through the lens of your wellness inquiry.

Dreams in Healing Systems the World Over

Except for in psychotherapy, modern Western medicine does not generally carve out a place for dreams. That is not true, though, when it comes to traditional healing systems that offer a more holistic and body-mind-spirit paradigm, including Ayurveda and traditional Chinese medicine, as well as the integrative medical approach known as homeopathy. Dreams also play a role in the healing approaches of many traditional cultures.

AYURVEDA

Ayurvedic medicine is a classical Indian healing system. Noting that *ayur* means "life" and *veda* means "wisdom" or "knowledge," it is seen as the science of life and longevity. Ayurveda honors the connection between mind, body, and spirit. It emphasizes the healing potential of diet, lifestyle habits, and nature-based medicine. While gaining popularity in the West in recent decades, it has longstanding roots in India, with the earliest texts on Ayurveda dating back thousands of years. Ayurveda notes that the character of our dreams is influenced by the quality and quantity of the sleep we have, itself influenced by our diet and lifestyle routines. Since ancient times, dreams were used in Ayurveda to offer insights on the diagnosis or prognosis of a disease. Dreams are referred to as *svapna* and thought to reflect the interweaving of four integral components: the physical body, mind, soul, and sense organs.

One way that Ayurveda addresses health is by ensuring that a person's unique temperament is balanced. There are three constitutions, also known as doshas: these are vata, pitta, and kapha. According to Ayurveda, dreams can be used to identify a person's dosha or see whether doshic imbalances currently exist.

- Vata dreams may include flying, climbing trees, and other general movements. They feature dry and arid environments, vivid images, and scenes that conjure anxiety.

- Pitta dreams may feature fire, lightning, the Sun, and the color gold. They may include action and adventure, as well as competition and conflict.

- Kapha dreams are more placid, and feature calming scenes in which nature or water may be highlighted. Birds, clouds, or milk may be included, and attachment is often a theme.

Another vantage point through which classic Ayurveda views dreams is their ability to infer the timing of an outcome of a prognostic dream. In one of the Ayurvedic texts, the *Harita Samhita*, it's noted that if the dream took place in the first part of the night, the results were to occur in one year; in the second part, in six months; in the third part, in three months; and in the fourth part, in ten days. It was also thought that pregnant women could get a sense of the gender of their baby in their dreams. For example, if a dream featured flowers such as lotus or water lily, the baby was likely to be a boy. Alternatively, if a dream included flowers such as rose or hibiscus, the woman was likely to give birth to a girl.

EXERCISE

Know Your Dosha

Interested in learning more about the intersection of Ayurveda and dreams? One of the first places to start is by learning which dosha (constitution) you are. While consulting with an Ayurvedic practitioner is the most thorough way to receive a dosha determination, you can also find quizzes online that will help you to understand which one you may be. Once you know your dosha, see whether your dreams accord with the qualities noted for each. If you track your dreams over time through this angle and find that your dosha-associated themes significantly shift, it may be signaling that your body and mind are somehow out of balance. As you make adjustments in your diet and pursue practices that reduce stress, see how that may be reflected in your dreams.

TRADITIONAL CHINESE MEDICINE

Traditional Chinese Medicine (TCM), which has been practiced for
thousands of years, has also gained prominence around the world in
the last decades for its holistic and efficacious approach. It features
body/mind practices such as acupuncture, herbal medicine, nutrition, tui
na massage, qi gong, and other modalities. TCM addresses the energetic flow of the
body, identifying different symptoms and emotions associated with each major organ.

Dreams are given high accord in this medical approach. They themselves are explained in
a unique way; as Giovanni Maciola shares in his book *The Practice of Chinese Medicine*,
dreams are due to the nighttime wanderings of the mind (known as the Ethereal Soul).
During the day, the Ethereal Soul resides in the liver, while at night when it moves to the
eyes, it inspires dreaming. TCM doctors usually ask about the frequency and nature of a
patient's dreams in order to further assess their health status. It's thought that a healthy
person should have sleep not disturbed by excessive dreams; although what excessive
constitutes isn't clear, some practitioners characterize it as frequent nightmares or anxious
dreams, or waking up exhausted after having many active dreams.

In the TCM classic text *The Yellow Emperor's Classic of Medicine*, it's noted that dreams
are influenced by the balance of the complementary, yet opposing, forces of yin and yang.
Another factor that's discussed is how dreams may reveal whether there exists an energy
deficiency or excess in one of five organs (liver, heart, spleen, lung, and kidney). According
to TCM, what you dream about can also be helpful for diagnosing health imbalances.
Within the ancient Chinese texts, you will find many dream images and what they represent
healthwise. For example, they note that if your liver is deficient in energy, your dreams
may include fragrant mushrooms or forests. If it's spring and you dream of lying under
a tree and are unable to get up, that may reflect liver deficiency; alternatively, dreams in
which you're angry may point to liver excess. Being immersed in water, swimming after
a shipwreck occurs, or overlooking an abyss are thought to reflect weak kidneys, while
if one dreams of volcanic eruptions in the summertime, it may signal that the dreamer's
heart is not strong. Different colors in dreams are thought to also reveal insights. Red is
associated with the heart; white, the lungs; black, the kidneys; green, the liver; and
yellow, the spleen.

MAASAI MEDICINE

The Maasai, an ethnic group who live in parts of Kenya and Tanzania, ascribe a lot of meaning to dreams, honoring them for their guidance and valuing them as a vital part of life. Morning rituals often include sharing dreams with those with whom you gather. Part of the approach that spiritual healers, known as *laiboni*, use to treat those seeking counsel is through interpreting their dreams. There are additional ways that dreams serve as founts for valuable insights: for example, according to Dr. Tanya Pergola in *Time Is Cows: Timeless Wisdom of the Maasai*, elders seeking more information about the sacred sites where they could potentially host an *orlpul* — a healing retreat — often look to their dreams to discover it.

YORÙBÁ MEDICINE

Also known as Orisha medicine, Yorùbá is a healing system popular in West Africa and the Caribbean. To help the community, traditional healers use a variety of techniques, including herbal medicine, the telling of folktales, intentional dancing, and dreams and dream interpretation. As the ancestors are thought to visit in a person's dream, Yorùbá healers receive healing wisdom from them in their oneiric visions. Additionally, the healer will not only ask their client about their recent dreams to try to further understand what may be ailing them, but they may also rely upon information that came through in their own dream for this aim. This can inform not only the diagnosis but also any helpful remedies and treatments that they may prescribe.

TIBETAN MEDICINE

Dreams have played an ongoing role in Tibetan medicine. Even before the arrival of Buddhism to Tibet in the seventh century, dream analysis maintained an integral role in medical knowledge as well as spiritual practice. Not only do physicians inquire about their patients' dreams, but they may also conjure a dream about them before their visits in hopes of attaining more insight into their prevailing condition. It's thought that dreams can be informative in all stages of a disease: before it manifests, during its process, and after it's been cured. Dream images are seen as representing symbolic snapshots of the parts of the body that may be infirmed.

Research into Health-Related Dreams

At this point, there is a dearth of scientific research into the intersectionality of dreams and health. That said, some exploration has been undertaken and has yielded fascinating results. One of the leading contributors to this realm was the Russian psychiatrist Vasily Kasatkin. Over a forty-year period, he created a database of over ten thousand dreams compiled from more than 1,200 people. Through analyzing their dreams, he found that many contained symbols that served as precursors to the development of illness; that illness-catalyzed dreams are filled with distress and are generally longer than other dreams; and that dreams can point toward the physical location of a disease. His findings are included in his book *Theory of Dreams*, which has recently been translated into English. In it, he notes, "Describe me the dream of a person and I will tell you what illness he suffers from."

Another person known for their research exploring how dreams may be related to illness is psychiatrist Robert Smith of Michigan State University. In the 1980s, he undertook two studies on the subject: "The Relationship of Dreaming and Being Ill" and "Dreams Reflect Biological Function." One of the striking findings suggested by his studies is that the severity and deterioration of a health condition is associated with themes portrayed in dreams. For example, he found that in men, it was dreams of death that correlated with the subsequent worsening of disease symptomology, while in women, it was dreams that featured themes of separation.

Another pioneer in the field is Patricia Garfield, PhD. One of the founders of the International Association for the Study of Dreams, Garfield has done a lot of exploration into the role that dreams play in health and well-being. In her book *The Healing Power of Dreams*, she recounts not only the role that dreams played in her own recovery from an injury, but also those of countless others whose oneiric visions provided them with diagnostic and therapeutic insights. In her book, she includes an amalgamation of numerous dream images and the health conditions with which they have been found to be associated.

Envisioning Your Health Through Dreams

This is not to say that every dream you have that features a certain image or scene means that you have an undiagnosed illness. Still, it may be interesting to pay close attention to your dreams to see if they offer you a compass that can further help you tune in to what you are experiencing on a somatic level. If you find yourself having a dream with a recurring theme, and you intuitively feel that it may be pointing to some underlying physiological weakness, consider discussing this with a doctor or other health-care professional. If you are under the weather, or dealing with a physical condition, remember the ability of dreams to provide us with under-the-radar wisdom. Listen in to your dreams to see if you can gather insights on how to bolster your health and well-being. Perhaps use this as a focus of your dream incubation, asking your oneiric visions to bring you awareness about curative suggestions that you could then research. Additionally, some people have noted that through lucid dreaming, they are able to overcome some underlying stress associated with health conditions that they may have. If this is of interest to you, consider consulting a health-care practitioner who practices lucid-dream therapy.

In the West, our vision of the healing potential of dreams is mostly limited to a psychotherapeutic perspective, rather than a somatic one. However, as more and more people turn to their dreams for insights, and we continue to move toward a health paradigm that embraces mind, body, and spirit, perhaps one day doctors will not only inquire about your sleep but will also routinely ask you, "How are your dreams?"

PART III:

dreamwork
practices

CHAPTER SIX

RECALLING YOUR DREAMS

As we know, dreams are mysterious and magical, inspiring and informative. They can provide us with answers to questions alluding us, give us awareness that may bolster our well-being, awe us with their imaginal wonder, and offer us access to a deep well of wisdom — that is, if we can remember them. Whether we want to undertake a concentrated dreamwork practice or we're just curious as to what was included in our nighttime musings, we need to remember our oneiric visions, bringing them to the awareness of our conscious mind. As much as there may be disagreement as to what dreams signify, there is definitely one thing that most everyone agrees upon: it's challenging to remember your dreams and not have them slip away.

One of the most frustrating things is waking up in the morning, being able to sense that you had a dream, and yet be unable to recall it. The dream feels at once so close, yet so far away. You know it's there, just right around some proverbial corner in your mind, and yet, you can't access it. Similarly frustrating — or for some, perhaps more so — is waking up with memory of a dream fragment, only to have it vaporize from your mind just moments later. To think that epics of reverie have occurred, to which you were present in a very special way, but which you can't bring to conscious memory, can be baffling, let alone disheartening. It feels like a tease, a cruel trick that someone is playing on us. Still, thankfully, there are tips and tricks that can help us more readily recall our dreams. Before we explore these, let's try to understand why it often seems like such a formidable task to remember our dreams.

Why Are Dreams So Hard to Remember?

Greek mythology offers us one vantage point, an archetypal lens through which to perceive this oneiric enigma. It turns out that the Greek god of sleep, Hypnos, lived in a cave by the River Lethe, a waterway famous for being a stream that inspired oblivion, as anyone who drank from it would soon forget their past. Reflecting this, it's as if when we sleep, we enter into a cavern in which forgetting seems to be the status quo and a natural part of the terrain we traverse. Mythology aside, let's look at some modern-day reflections that may help us understand why remembering our dreams can be so challenging.

IT'S A MATTER OF TIME

Part of the reason that we forget our dreams may come down to a numbers game. It's been noted that our dreams disappear rather quickly when we transition from sleeping to waking. On average, within 5 minutes, we forget 50 percent of what we dream; within 10 minutes, only 10 percent may remain. Given this, if we don't set about to capture them soon after we awaken, they may drift away and be exceptionally difficult to reclaim.

DREAMS DEFY THE ORDINARY

We spend much of our waking days using left-brain thinking, addressing and processing ideas in a rational, analytical, and linear fashion. But dreams are different, bastions of the fantastical that often defy daytime-consensus reality. As such, it may take effort for us to get our head around what we just perceived, not necessarily readily having the words to describe the seemingly illogical events that we just witnessed. Plus, while some dreams may feature conversations, our oneiric adventures are heavily visual. For many people, trying to quickly translate these visual images — which may seem nonsensical, and therefore, hard to define into words — may be a difficult experience. We struggle to do so, and as time ticks away, our ability to remember them slips away.

THE BARRIER OF OUR BRAIN CHEMISTRY

The work of sleep scientists may help us to further understand just why it's so difficult to remember our dreams. There are certain neurotransmitters (brain chemicals) necessary to transform short-term memories into long-term ones; some of these — including norepinephrine — are at a very low level while we're dreaming, therefore creating an innate blockade to having our nighttime visions etched into our mind. The shift of brain chemistry, and the concurrent fluctuations in the activity of different brain regions that occurs as we move between waking, sleeping, and dreaming, may provide us with clues about why our physiology inherently restricts us from readily remembering our dreams.

THE COST OF COMPROMISED SLEEP

The dreams that arrive in the early morning hours are thought to be more vivid and complex, given that at this point, the REM sleep stage — known for producing more highly activated and visual dreams — lasts longer. Therefore, those who are short sleepers, including those who have sleep-maintenance insomnia and wake up early and can't fall back to sleep, may miss out on these dreams. And since their heightened vividness and emotional saliency make them so stirring and memorable, it may be that we're not remembering our dreams because we're not having these highly impressionable ones.

THE STRENGTH OF AVOIDANCE

Some posit that dreams are repositories for the thoughts and feelings that we brush aside during the day, those that we avoid facing. If our dreams contain unacknowledged aspects of ourselves that we tried to initially avoid, it would make sense that we may have built-in defenses that would work hard to keep them at bay from our conscious mind. It then follows that if we want to keep the premise of "out of sight, out of mind" alive, we could create resistance to remembering our dreams. Relatedly, if we had nightmares as a child, or other experiences that had us associating dreams with negative experiences, we may do whatever we can to try to push away our oneiric memories so that we don't have to encounter them.

Who's More Apt to Remember Their Dreams?

Some people can regularly recall the finest details of their dreams, while others awaken with no memory at all, even questioning whether they've had a dream. What determines whether someone can remember their dreams is something that medical researchers have been interested in for quite some time, with their work unearthing numerous significant and interesting discoveries. Understanding what may differentiate those who are high- versus low-recallers can be of great guidance if we want to further forge our oneiric recollection skills and take our recall game to the next level. Characteristics of those who more regularly recall their dreams include the following.

THEY ACKNOWLEDGE THE VALUE OF THEIR DREAMS

Not surprisingly, those who revere their dreams and accept them as an integral part of their life remember them more often. Those in cultures around the world, and throughout history, that value dreams as an important periscope into knowledge display a greater ability to bring them forth into the waking world. And those who regularly share their dreams with others — whether it be their partner, friends, relatives, or community members — have been found to have greater access to their dreams. Similarly, research suggests that those who have more confidence that they can remember them actually do.

THEY ARE MORE SENSITIVE AND OPEN TO NEW EXPERIENCES

High dream recallers may also be more likely to have certain personality traits. The characteristic known as openness — in which someone is more motivated and capable of adapting to new experiences — has been linked to better dream recall. Those who are sensitive and have thinner personal boundaries have also been found to remember their dreams more often. Not surprisingly, those who struggle to find words to describe their feelings seem to recall their dreams less frequently.

THEY ARE IMAGINATIVE

Those who are creative and imaginative also tend to remember their dreams more often. Since they contain a concentrated pictorial element, it's not surprising that visual learners, creatives, and those more sensitive to aesthetics have been found to have better recall.

THEY ARE INTROSPECTIVE

Dreamers who regularly tune in to their inner world have been found to have better recall. These include people who have meditation and contemplative practices, as well as those who are in therapy. People who are highly oriented to their imaginal life — whether through daydreaming or letting their imaginations soar — are also more apt to remember their dreams.

THEY GET ADEQUATE SLEEP

It would also make sense that those who get more sleep are more apt to remember their dreams for the sheer reason that there are more of them to possibly recall. Plus, as we've seen, early morning REM periods are longer and provide us with an extended opportunity to have vivid dreams. Given that such dreams may be more intricate, they may also be more memorable.

THEY TEND TO BE YOUNGER AND FEMALE

Research has found that dream recall peaks in early adulthood and declines from there on, notably lower in older age. Whether this is biologically based or a reflection of a decreasing interest in dreams and their introspective nature is not clear. Women seem to remember their dreams more than men do; the reason for this is uncertain, although it could relate to the fact that women, generally speaking, tend to be more emotionally focused than men and seek to understand their feelings (something that dreams can offer).

General Recall Strategies

Based upon these research findings, we can create strategies that may help our dream recall.

BELIEVE IN THE VALUE OF YOUR DREAMS

The fact that you're reading this book already puts you at an advantage, since it reflects your interest — or at least a concentrated curiosity — to more deeply connect with your dreams and all that they may offer you. Continuing to advocate for their role in your life and well-being may help you to remember them more often. Additionally, being grateful for what they reveal — whether something practical or just fascinating — is a sign of reverence, which we have seen is a factor that helps to amplify recall. Similarly, following breakthrough solutions that a dream contains lets it know that you honor it.

HAVE CONFIDENCE YOU'LL REMEMBER THE DREAM

When you go to sleep at night, tell yourself you will remember your oneiric visions. Think of yourself as someone who not only has dreams — we all do — but someone who can bring memories of them forward into the waking world. Even on days that you don't remember anything or even very little, remind yourself that that's OK and doesn't mean that you won't access more tomorrow. On those days, still continue to make an entry into your dream journal, noting, "I had dreams, although I don't remember them right now."

GET GOOD SLEEP

You can add remembering your dreams to the list of the many benefits that having adequate sleep yields. Those who have sufficient sleep invariably have more REM sleep, and a greater concentration of the more vivid and memorable dreams that occur in this slumber stage. Make a concerted effort to aim for your target sleep goals; for most adults, that's 7-plus hours each night.

CURATE YOUR CREATIVITY

Exposing yourself to more visual images during the day will help exercise the associated part of your brain, enhancing your facility to experience the world this way. Appreciate the image itself, perceiving all of its nuances. Allocate time to writing about some images you see, describing them as clearly as you can; this will allow you to further develop a link between what you see and the words that can describe it, a skill inherently important for capturing your dreams. Also, inspire your right brain by reading poetry. This type of prose is usually nonlinear in its wayfinding. As such, it's similar to dreams and may allow your mind to start thinking more in this manner.

CONNECT TO YOUR FEELINGS

Being more connected to our feelings has many benefits, not the least being that it may help us to remember our dreams. If we're open to the emotions that may arise, knowing we have the capacity to deal with what may come, it helps us better remember what was carried forth in our oneiric visions.

Similarly, spending more time being introspective may also be of benefit. Take a quiet walk, relax in a bath while listening to music, let yourself daydream. If you don't have a meditation practice, start one.

BE MORE OPEN-MINDED

Being more adaptable, curious, and open to adventure is a way of orienting that has many benefits, including greater oneiric recall. Try to be more amenable to surprises and detours (something with which dreams are filled), knowing that they sometimes put you on a path that yields unexpected, and beneficial, experiences and insights.

TALK ABOUT YOUR DREAMS

Find friends, family, or colleagues to talk to about your dreams. See if your partner or your child is interested in a morning check-in, with each person asking the other how their dreams were. Explore dream groups in your area, or start one. Having an encouraging social context will help you to remember them more often.

Tips for Enhanced Dream Recall

Try the tips below if you are having trouble remembering your dreams.

- Don't judge any images that come forth. Just allow them to arise. Resist resisting what may surface. In general, at this point, you don't want to play editor; rather, you want to assume the role of an inviting audience, witnessing all that is occurring.

- Remember that you may recall a story line or perhaps one or several images, or both. One is not better than the other: be open to what comes through. If you remember even one detail, don't discount its value. Stay with it. Let it marinate.

- Tune in to how you feel when you awaken. Even if you can't access images, knowing the feeling state that the dream inspired is of great value. Tune in to how the dream felt.

- If you're not readily able to access dream images or a story line, scan through the faces of people to whom you're emotionally connected. They may have been represented in your dream, and this may trigger a memory. Additionally, since many dreams are strongly influenced by our recent waking experiences, survey your previous day and see if any event that occurred sparks a dream memory.

- Once images and/or a story line appear, go back over them again and again in your mind, to assist in etching them into your memory. Remember that while the first set of impressions you receive are, in and of themselves, exceptionally valuable, they will likely lead to your ability to mine for others that are connected to them.

- No matter how much you remember, document it. If you don't remember anything, just note that. By doing so, you'll emphasize your belief that, in fact, you do have dreams. This will allow for the unbroken continuation of your dream-capturing routine.

- Create a set of small note cards that contain the name of the images, symbols, places, or words that occur frequently in your dreams. After you've spent your first several minutes awake being quiet with your eyes closed, you can then look at the cards and see if they trigger a memory of anything that occurred in your dream.

Recall Rituals

Here are some time-honored practices that can heighten your ability to consciously connect to the dreams you've had.

Before Bed

1   Make sure that the tools you're going to use capture your dreams — whether paper and pen, audio recorder, or something else — are easily accessible by your bedside.

2   Some people find that reflecting upon their day backward helps them to then go back into their dreams when they wake up. To do so, as you're relaxing before you doze off, visualize yourself in bed, then think about what you did just before getting into bed, what occurred before then, and before then, taking yourself on a quick tour of your day, from finish to start. This practice can help you in the morning, as you'll be readily primed to take a back-in-time orientation and look to see what oneiric visions just recently arose in your mind.

3   As you relax to fall asleep, tell yourself that you will have dreams while you're sleeping, and that you will remember them in the morning.

69

<u>**4**</u> Practice dream incubation, in which you contemplate the insights and solutions that you'd like your dream to include. In addition to helping you to access key problem-solving and creative insights, this technique hones intention, which can enhance recall. Remind yourself that when you wake up in the morning, you will relax in bed for a few minutes so that you can capture your dream.

Upon Awakening

<u>**1**</u> Be leisurely when you awaken. Don't jump out of bed, nor feel a sense of pressure that you need to begin your day immediately. You're still in the liminal space between sleeping and waking, and the connection to the dream is still strong.

<u>**2**</u> This can help you to access and bring them back to consciousness. Remember, the first 5 to 10 minutes provide you with the most opportune time for recalling your dreams.

<u>**3**</u> If the position you generally sleep in is different than the one in which you wake up, gently go back to your slumbering position, as this will connect you to what's known as state-dependent memory. Doing so may help you to access your dreams.

CHAPTER SEVEN

DOCUMENTING YOUR DREAMS

Now that you're armed with strategies to enhance your dream recall, let's explore the next important stage in working with your dreams: capturing and documenting them. For some people, remembering their dreams each night is rewarding enough. Just the process of recalling them and giving them voice satisfies a desire to acknowledge what the dream brought forth. Others like to collect and organize their dreams in a capsule, a dream journal in which they can take up residence, and from which they can be read and reread, worked through to yield the wealth of insights that they can offer.

For those who like to collect them in a cache, some like to write down their dreams directly into their journals as they're remembering them. Others, though, find that they like to have an intermediate step, one in which they first capture their dream and then transcribe it into their journal afterward, finding this helps them be more methodical as they unpack their dream's meaning. Regardless of whether you're a one- or multi-step dream journaler, this chapter will provide you with tips and tidbits that will augment this process for you. Remember that when it comes to dreamwork, there's no one-size-fits-all approach. Explore the techniques within this chapter, seeing which ones may serve you in your dreamwork practice.

Capturing Your Dreams

Using the dream-catching strategies discussed in the previous chapter, you'll be able to tap into initial memories of your nighttime visions. As they coalesce in your mind, the next step is to glean and capture them, shuttling what you've recollected — whether an entire story line or just even an image or a feeling — out of your mind and into documented form. Writing down dreams is the standard approach, but numerous other strategies also can be helpful, depending upon the unique style through which you process information.

Regardless of which method you choose, it's important to not judge or edit yourself when you're trying to bring forth your dreams. Record everything that comes to you, whether or not it seems to make sense. Don't worry about getting the sequence right when you first record your dreams; just document everything that you recall initially, knowing that you will string things together in a more formal way later on. Even if what you're remembering doesn't seem especially cogent, you may find that these threads of memory eventually will lead you down a path that connects you to other details that you didn't initially access. This is one of the reasons that many people find it beneficial to record their dreams in two stages: (1) the initial capturing stage, when you first wake up; and (2) the subsequent phase when you document them, transferring your recollections to a journal and further organizing and working with them. Not feeling the pressure to get your dream first scribed in a certain systematic (or even tidy) way will give you more freedom and disengage the censoring you may be otherwise inclined to do. This allows you unencumbered connection to your dream memory while it's still fresh in your mind.

Also, try not to interpret your dreams as you're first trying to capture them, as this, too, can thwart your ability to remember precious insights. There will be lots of time to analyze and interpret them later. This first phase is the fact-finding stage and we want to mine and recover as much treasure as we can. Here are several approaches for initially capturing your dreams. Unless you have a tried-and-true method, consider experimenting with these, seeing which works better for you. Also, you don't have to choose just one. You may find that a combination works for you, or that some fit better with certain styles of dreams or at different times in your life.

WRITING

Most people capture their dreams by jotting them down on paper. And while writing them immediately into a dream journal may be standard fare, as previously noted, some people find this approach to have a restrictive drawback; this may arise from numerous factors, including that their middle-of-the-night handwriting may not necessarily be all that legible and in a form that they want to have preserved forever in their journal.

Additionally, feeling that they want their journal to be neat and orderly may have them place undue pressure on themselves when writing down their dream images, which could stifle the spontaneity of what is arising.

A great workaround? Instead of first writing in your journal, record your dreams on paper that you keep by your bedside. This can be a small pad, notebook, index cards, a loose sheet of paper — anything that has a shape and size that allows you to easily write. Record all that you can on this paper, and then later transcribe it into your dream journal.

Of course, you'll need a good writing instrument. Have one that writes really easily, in which you take pleasure using. Make sure before you go to bed that it has ink in it, or if it's a pencil, that it's sharpened. After all, you want to avoid the commonplace frustration of having access to a bevy of dream memories ready to be transcribed, only to not be able to do so because of a dried-up pen or blunted pencil.

Given that you may awaken in the middle of the night and want to write your dreams, having a light source is also important. Best is a hands-free headlight, a pen that has a light attached, or a book light attached to your notebook. The light should be strong enough to see by, yet not too illuminative to be jarring or stimulating, to yourself or your bed partner.

Some people find that typing their dreams into the notes section of their phone or tablet works as a good method. Others, however, find that there's more of a chance for spelling mistakes to occur, and that it ends up making the dream record less decipherable. Plus, if you end up spending time correcting typos or erroneous autocorrects along the way, you may find that it eats into the precious moments you initially have while your dreams are still fresh in your mind. In addition, if you're logging dreams in the middle of the night, you want to avoid the melatonin-stymieing blue light from tech screens, as it can lead to subsequent sleep disruption. The other disadvantage to this approach is reflected

in the benefit of handwriting: the process of putting pen to paper
helps us to allocate things to memory better than does typing.
All said, though, if you've found this system works for you, then
continue to use it.

DRAWING

Sometimes it's really hard to capture dreams in writing; after all, they
are so visual. In these cases, give yourself the freedom to draw, as it's a great way to fish
out dream images and feelings. You can draw anything from the dream — you need not
limit yourself to just diagramming an image. You may even find that scribbling lines on a
paper helps you to capture a scene's layout. Or, if you remember a certain color that casts
a hue throughout the dream, you can use a colored pencil or marker to represent it.

Doodling is really helpful, too, as sometimes you may not be able to access images,
but can readily tap into the feelings elicited by the dream and express them in uniquely
formed lines and shapes. Since dreams are often not linear and don't mirror the
arrangement of space to which we're accustomed, doodling them may give you more
boundless freedom to connect to them.

A pictorial approach can also be used to express the sequence of events, drawing small
scenes one after the other. You may find that sometimes just allowing yourself to draw
a shape that feels related to your dream will trigger a greater memory of what occurred,
whether at the moment or later on. Remember that what you draw need not be a work of
art, or even something recognizable. Don't judge yourself; just let yourself be free. Don't
worry about being a Picasso; whatever you can get on paper has exceptional value.

AUDIO RECORDING

Even if you're a fast writer, sometimes you may find that the pace of your writing is
slower than necessary to document all of the details that come forth when you remember
a dream. A great workaround for this is to audio record your oneiric memories. You don't
even need to get a new device, as many phones come with a preinstalled voice-recording
app. And if yours doesn't, don't worry: there are scores that can be purchased and
downloaded, some even for free. It's amazing how much more quickly most people can

speak their dreams than write them. And since we know that time is key, because they dissipate so quickly, recording them may help you to access and preserve more of them.

There may be another benefit as well; after all, when we first awaken from slumber, and our muscles are regaining the coordination they lost during sleep, our handwriting may not be at its peak. Our voice, though, even if it's muffled, is still pretty recognizable. Perhaps you've had that experience of feeling really excited that you remembered a dream and wrote it down, only to later feel so frustrated when you were unable to make heads or tails of it; audio recording it is a way to sidestep this possibility.

For privacy purposes, you likely won't want to have your recorded dreams on your phone for too long, unless you regularly use a password to guard access. As such, you can even opt to send it right away to your computer, or upload it to cloud storage, and then erase it before you transcribe it in your journal. Don't forget to give it a title that includes the date so that you can readily find it.

This approach may be tricky if you share a bed with someone and you awaken before they do. Not only, of course, will speaking out loud rouse them, but it may also infringe upon your privacy. As such, you may need to quickly steal away to the bathroom or another secluded spot to record your dreams. This approach may work fine in the morning, although it might not end up being the best strategy for middle-of-the-night recalls, given that shuffling out of bed could be jarring and impinge upon your ability to get back to sleep. If that's the case for you, then you may want to opt instead for jotting or drawing your middle-of-the-night dream memories.

VIDEO RECORDING

Some people like to capture some of their dreams in video format. With this method, you get to not only record the audio but also some of the visual components of your oneiric visions. Video also allows you to reflect the emotions that the dream evoked through capturing your facial expressions or movements. Remember, you don't have to keep the video for time immemorial; it's just a tool for you to document the initial memories of your dreams. Once you transcribe the video into words, you can then delete it. No special equipment is needed for this method; just use the video feature on your smartphone's camera.

DREAM JOURNALING APPS

Another way to document your dreams is to do so with an app, which you can use on either your phone or tablet. The features of apps range, but at their heart, they include a diary in which you can type your dream. Many also include the ability to add tags to further code them. There are also apps designed for lucid dreamers, which not only feature tips and techniques but also alarms and notification functions that can remind you to do reality checks. If you want to tap into a community of virtual dreamers, some apps feature a database of users' dreams that you can search through to read and/or comment upon.

Say Your Dreams Aloud

Sometimes, saying a dream aloud helps you to better remember it. If you share a bed with someone, and it feels right, you can share your dream with each other when you wake up. Speaking your dream can help to make it conscious and commit it to memory. Plus, sharing dreams may be a sweet ritual to do with someone with whom you are intimate. This ritual is a nod to ones done in more traditional communities, wherein dreams would be listened to by the tribe or a trusted advisor.

Capture What You Can

There may be times when you remember an epic amount of your dream and have the time to write it down immediately. There may be other times, though, when you don't have that luxury, either because you can't access that much of your dream or you need to get out of bed pretty quickly. There may also be times when you need to further jog your memory a bit to be able to net even a whisper of what transpired. If you don't have much time and/or you can't initially remember that much, still, try to spend a couple of minutes to write down what you remember. Consider doing one of these exercises, which will help you to scribe some oneiric souvenirs.

Seven Words

Write down seven words that feel connected to your dream. These could be related to things that happened, symbols that appeared, or the tone that wove itself through. Aim for seven words, but if you can't access that target, write as many as you can.

Connect to the Feeling

Jot down how you feel upon waking, what your mood is like. And if you can remember the feeling tone of your dream, note that as well.

Body Orientation

Scan your body and see whether your attention focuses in on any specific area. Consider whether your dream featured that part, or parts, of your body as a key image. Document any pertinent information.

The 4 Ws

Quickly jot the signature aspects of your dream, from a Who, Where, What, and When perspective.

Who: The main characters

Where: Description of the location or locations

What: A few notes about what transpired

When: Identify the time — whether in general as past, present, future — or more specifically, if you can, in which the dream took place.

Dream Documenting

Putting all your dreams in one place — a journal, for example — allows you to keep them organized so that you can return to them at a later time, reviewing and finding more meaning within them, whether in a single dream or across several of them. And even if you don't return to your dreams regularly, or ever again, just knowing that they are recorded imbues them with reverence and a sense of validity. It encourages them to take on the feel of a documentary of your life, or part of your life.

And there is also the other benefit of this two-stage process, where you initially capture your dreams and then later transcribe them in a journal: it gives you another opportunity to remember possibly forgotten details. The process of transferring them from their initial state — whether written, drawn, voice recorded, or video recorded — gives you an additional chance to bring forth more possibly forgotten facets of the dream, allowing you to unearth more awareness as to what it revealed than you may have initially considered.

It's recommended to have a section within each journal entry where you write your unedited notes and recollections. You will use these initial memories that you captured in the steps just outlined to further detail and decipher your dreams. Here are some tips for documenting your dreams, transferring them from their originally captured form to your journal repository.

WHEN

Have this practice be one that has as much consistency as feels right. Consider blocking off some time each day to doing so. If that doesn't work for you, you can allocate several days a week to transcribe your dream notes into your journal. If you do it each day, it can be just after you've captured them, or later on. You can do this step separate from the next one, in which you further work and decode the dream, or during the same time frame.

Allocate a period of time in which you have adequate ability to do this. Make sure you won't have interruptions. Prepare some coffee or tea, play some music, and/or light candles. Do whatever feels right to make this a relaxing and enjoyable practice. This process can take as much or as little time as you want and have. Don't feel pressured to consistently have it be a dedicated activity. Even just spending 5 minutes to initially document your dreams in your journal will be a significant step in the process.

WHERE

While you can do this activity anywhere, consider allocating a dedicated space to doing it, as this will make it more of a ritual. It can be at your desk, the kitchen table, a chair in the living room, a cushion by your dream altar, your bathtub, or any other place that feels nurturing to you. If you associate this spot with reflection work, once you arrive there, you will feel more attuned to slowing down, being inwardly quiet, and getting into a dreamier space. Have it be someplace where you can have privacy and quiet, whether it's a room that has a door or a spot that you know won't be used by anyone else in the family at a certain time. Keep your dreamwork supplies there; this, of course, includes your journal, but may also include items such as writing and drawing instruments (markers, colored pencils, pastels, and the like), as well as scrapbooking/collaging items (such as magazines, scissors, glue, etc.) if you want to have your journal feature multi-media representations of your dreams.

HOW

The first step is to transcribe or add your dream recollections to your journal in an unfiltered way. As previously noted, it's always good to have a section in your journal that just features the raw material, the original capture, of your dream.

If you captured your dream in written words, transcribe them in your journal. If you captured your dream in pictures, you can do one of two things: redraw them in your journal or affix the originals with tape.

If you captured your dream in audio form, transcribe what you said into words. If you're using a computer-based dream journal, you can even use transcription software to do so, although make sure to read it over afterward. This is important for two reasons: you don't want there to be any misinterpretations, and you want the opportunity to reconnect with your dreams at this point.

If you captured your dream in video, transcribe the audio portion into words. If you're using a paper dream journal, describe in words the movements you made or the facial expressions you used. If you're using a digital dream journal, you may be able to import the video and integrate it as part of the entry record.

As you begin to transfer your notes, you may find that you can remember more of the dream. One image may lead to another, or you may see how some of the things you recall string together with others.

Next Steps

After you've transcribed your initial recollections in your dream journal, you can begin to survey your dreams to further access the layers of wisdom that they have afforded you. One of the key steps in decoding your dreams — understanding individual ones as well as groups of them — is to identify the different components that they include, as well as attributes that they have. This is something that you can easily do by organizing the pages of your dream journal in a certain way, and something that we'll explore in the next chapter.

To Sleep, or to Record a Dream?

Given that most of us have four to five periods of vivid dream potential through a night's sleep, there are numerous opportunities to capture our dreams. Some dreamers may have no qualms about grabbing their journal in the middle of the night should they arise mid-sleep to write down the whispers of their oneiric visions. And lucid dreamers who practice the Wake Back to Bed method may even intentionally set their alarm clocks to wake them up in the early morning hours; this way, they can not only record a dream, but also stay awake and practice techniques that may foster their lucidity. And yet, there may be times that you arise from a dream and would rather turn over to go back to sleep than turn on the light and write in your journal. There's no right or wrong; do what feels aligned with your dream inquiry quest, as well as the ways in which you know you need to tap into your rest.

More Documenting Tips

As you're documenting your dreams, you have yet another opportunity to remember more of them. Here are some additional dream-mining activities to consider:

- If you remember a movement that occurred in your dream, act it out. This proprioceptive experience may help trigger other dream memories.

- If a line from a song appeared in your dream, listen to the entire song to see whether it jogs your memory of your dream or gives you more context as to why it was included.

- If you use the tarot as a tool for divining insights, pick a card while intentioning that it will help you connect to something in your dream you may not have yet remembered. Survey the card and look at its entire gestalt, as well as the individual images, design dynamics, the name of the card, and even its number. It's easiest to do this exercise using only the twenty-two Major Arcana cards.

CHAPTER EIGHT

USING A DREAM JOURNAL

For many, their dream journal is the centerpiece of their dreamwork practice, a capsule in which their oneiric odysseys are preserved. A dream journal serves as a looking-glass chronicle through which we can reconnect to the hopes, wishes, fears, and concerns that channel through our minds and hearts, which are uniquely revealed during the night when we sleep and dream. Our dream journals are replete with autobiographical reflections that help us to know ourselves better, all the while also having us remember the exquisite power that emerges when we tap into our imaginal mind. In addition to being a coffer of self-awareness treasures, our dream journals not only serve as the destination for our insights, but also as a tool that helps us to discover the wisdom that our dreams yield.

83

The Array of Dream Journals

There are numerous dream journals available. While some feature beautiful covers and inspirational quotes, there are others that are designed to help encourage you to remember your dreams and record them in ways in which you can access their deeper levels. Some come complete with section headings ready-made for you to scribe the date, title, and some visual notes, while others include journaling prompts, checkboxes to help you describe the dream, and spaces dedicated to both recording and reflecting upon it. If you've not found a dream journal that's visually appealing, helps you to stay motivated, and also acts as a guide to help unearth what your dreams may mean, there's another option: you can create your own. It's not difficult nor time-consuming, and it can be one of the most powerful steps you can take to connect to the heart of the wisdom that your dreams contain.

All it requires is creating different sections in your journal pages, areas that help you to organize some of your dream details in a way that mirrors your interests and meets your needs. It's a powerful tool to help you zero in on the numerous facets of your dreams and further understand just what they may mean. This chapter will give you some tips and strategies that can boost your journaling practice to take your dreamwork to the next level.

Types of Journals

Before we get into the details on how to make a customized journal that addresses the things that you're most interested in assessing and analyzing, let's start at the beginning, and consider what type of book to use. There are generally two basic options from which to choose. Regardless of which you select, choose a size that will work best for you in terms of providing you a good amount of space to write. Even if you don't use it all, not feeling constrained may open up the channel to your memory; it's a way of sending a message to your subconscious mind that you know that there is something vast that wants to be shared and understood, and that you're giving yourself adequate space where it can be documented. By doing so, you're imparting a greater sense of possibility and encouragement, which can inspire a better ability to understand the vast layers of your dream.

NOTEBOOK

There are a range of notebook possibilities from which to choose. You could use a simple spiral-bound book. Or, you could opt for a bound notebook; if so, find one that lies flat when opening it, as you'll soon see how instrumental working with facing pages is. For most people, blank pages offer more freedom of expression than ones that are lined, allowing them to also have a space to draw or doodle if they choose. Others prefer those that are dotted, as this helps them to make lines to readily demarcate different sections. See what works best for your particular journaling style. Given that you'll want to number the pages, if it already has page numbers printed on it, that can be a plus. As you'll soon see, if you choose to use a notebook, you'll be making space on each page for different sections in which you will fill in an array of information related to your dreams.

BINDER BOOK

Another approach is to create templated pages on the computer, print them out, three-hole punch them, and keep them in a binder. You'd print them on two sides, with each page having a different layout on the front and back. This allows you to not only record and organize different aspects of your dreams but also take advantage of there being facing pages with which to work. Like with the notebook option, make sure that the binder opens flat for ease of use.

Dream Journal Page Designs

Designing your own dream journal is not only easy and creative, but it can also help you to access deeper levels of insights. Whether you want a design that lets you capture the basics or a bespoke one that allows you to track a variety of different dream variables that may be of interest, in the following pages you'll find suggestions on how to organize your journal to optimize your dreamwork.

As you'll see, in each of these layout options, I suggest that instead of having each night's dream featured on subsequent pages, that you allocate two facing pages — one of the left and one on the right side of your journal — for each dream. Not only does this expansive space give your psyche a sense of freedom so that it doesn't feel limited as to what it can capture and document, but it also inspires your ability to make more connections. One of my favorite ways to use these facing pages, and which serves as the foundation for my approach, is to document initial memories of a dream on the left-side page and scribe reflections on the dream's significance on the right-side page. Being able to see both your dream memories and your reflections at once enables a dialogue that not only engages your mind, but can also bring through originally forgotten dream details. It's a much easier and more efficient approach than having to flip back and forth between pages that contain information on the same dream. And there's another benefit: if you're someone who likes to write their dream directly into their journal rather than take an intermediate step (as we discussed in the last chapter), having a dedicated space that's separate from any evaluation or reflection can help you keep your dream journal more organized.

BASIC JOURNAL DESIGN

The basic dream journal design suits many people quite well. For the basic one, you just need a space for the following information, which you arrange on facing pages.

Date: Including the date you had the dream is, of course, essential. Given that we often don't know the exact moment we had a dream, and we may be interested in understanding our dream in the context of the previous day's events, consider including the dates of both the evening you went to bed and the morning you awoke in your journal.

Memories: Allocate a good portion of the left-hand page for documenting all that you recalled from your dream. You can either write directly in here as you're recalling your dream or transcribe what you originally wrote elsewhere, or what you audio or video recorded when you first arose.

Reflections: This is the section in which you document what you feel the dream signifies. It's where you record your ongoing thoughts on the different layers of the dream, and what message it may be offering you.

Page Number: Numbering the pages will allow you to create a Table of Contents so that you can readily rediscover a dream you had.

Title: Giving your dream a title can help you to further distill its meaning and significance. You can also use it in your journal's Table of Contents when cataloging your dreams. Additionally, giving it a title is another opportunity to express your creativity in your dreamwork.

BESPOKE JOURNAL DESIGN

While the basic design works great, you may find that you want to capture other details related to your dreams. Including additional categories of information will not only make your dream journal richer, but it will also further enhance your ability to see what your dreams may be revealing. Plus, it's a great system to help you understand patterns that may weave throughout your dreams.

Here are some ideas of categories that you can include in your dream journal. Experiment with the ones that seem most interesting; you need not use all of them. Try different ones at different times to see which ones help you to best connect with your dreams and understand what they mean. Of course, this isn't an exhaustive list. As you continue to work with your dreams, you may find additional subjects that are of interest that you may want to include.

Feelings

Dreams often have an emotional tone. Sometimes it's even easier to connect with the feeling tone of the dream than it is to recover the who, what, where, and when details that it featured. Additionally, as our dreams are often related to the processing of opportunities and challenges from our waking life — and the related emotions that they bring forth — what we were feeling before we fell asleep often informs our dreams.

And as we know, the demarcation between dreaming and waking isn't that stringent. Often what is catalyzed in our dreams infuses itself into our waking awareness afterward, sometimes with such tenacity that it feels hard to shake off the emotional residue that a dream imparted. As such, questions that address our feelings may yield interesting insights. Consider adding a section to your journal with the following or similar questions. You can even fill out the first one before you fall asleep.

■ How did I feel when I went to bed?

■ What feelings arose in my dreams?

■ How do I feel upon arising?

■ How do I feel after exploring my dreams?

Day's Reflections

Our days and nights weave together, forming the whole tapestry of who we are. Our dreams often reflect our digesting and absorbing the ideas, situations, and feelings that occurred the preceding day. As such, noting daily occurrences may help us to further understand our dreams. Consider including these prompts in your dream journal. You could, of course, answer these questions the night before you go to sleep; just change the orientation of the questions if you do.

- What was I grateful for yesterday?
- What did I worry about yesterday?
- What significant events, if any, transpired yesterday?

Dream Incubation Intention

Dream incubation is a practice in which you intentionally ask your dream to reveal specific insights that are of import to you. If you are incubating a dream, it's helpful to include the intention in your journal before you go to sleep. This, of course, helps you keep a record of it, and then hones your focus in the morning when you begin to discern what your dream revealed about your query. It also provides another benefit: it's not uncommon to have created the most powerful dream intention as you're unwinding in bed, only to not remember it the next morning.

- Dream incubation intention

Symbols, Images, and Themes

Dreams are rich in symbols, images, and themes that weave throughout. Sometimes we may not even remember the narrative of our dreams, although we can readily recall the iconic visuals that were included within. The images may be those whose meaning is obvious, or they may be rife with substrata of unique meanings that take time to access. These symbols, images, and themes may include anything in the dream that you found striking, whether obtusely mundane or bizarrely out of the ordinary. Note any colors or numbers that may have appeared. If you remember seeing or hearing words, record those as well.

Unpacking the significance of what a dream symbol means can be a fascinating foundation of our dreamwork, as we come to learn how it speaks to us and reflects the complex weave of who we are. As such, consider adding a section in your journal that highlights the symbols and images that were featured in your dreams. You could have themes woven in there or featured as a separate section.

- Symbols and images
- Themes

Outcomes Inspired

As we reflect upon our dreams, we may find that we get some really powerful takeaways. Some of these may even point us toward actions we feel we are ready to embark upon. Including these in your dream journal will serve as another testament to the healing and wisdom-inspiring benefits that dreams have in your life.

- Takeaways
- Outcomes inspired

Digital Dream Journals

Traditionally, a reference to a dream journal infers a paper book, whether one that is hard- or spiral-bound. These allow you to write and draw by hand, as well as customize with collages or stickers, and include found objects that feel connected to a dream. However, a dream journal doesn't have to be analog. It can also be created on a digital medium. You can create one using your computer's word-processing software or an online platform that allows you to weave words with digital media.

Sleeping Environment

The more you do dreamwork, the more you may come to see that certain factors influence the type of dreams you have, and their quality and contents. Some of these may center upon your sleeping environs, as well as factors that influenced your slumber. By tracking these, you may begin to see further interlacing patterns that are not only interesting but also informative. For example, you could include such questions as the following in your dream journal.

- How many hours of sleep did I have?
- How was the quality of my sleep?
- What was I thinking about when I went to sleep?
- Where did I sleep?
- With whom did I sleep?
- Did I have sex before I went to sleep?
- Did I awaken in the night?
- At what approximate time did the dream occur?

Lucid Dreaming

If you lucid dream, you can also track important information in your journal that can help to enhance your practice, let alone allow you to document your awareness-filled adventures. This can include not only details of your oneiric journeys, but also the dream signs you recognized and techniques that you used to foster the dream.

- The sign/s that let me recognize I was in a lucid dream
- The lucid-dreaming techniques I used last night

AstroDreamwork

For those who are interested in weaving together astrological insights with their dreamwork, you can include additional variables in your journal. These may comprise the phase and/or sign of the Moon, the current astrological passages/transits through which you're moving, or anything else that you find provides you clues as to the meaning of your dreams.

- Moon phase
- Moon sign
- Current astrological passages/ transits

PATTERN RECOGNITION

Not only does having categorized sections in your dream journal allow you to dig into them deeper, but it also helps you to recognize patterns that may exist. For example, if you track the images that appear in your dreams and also what you were thinking about before you fell asleep, you may be able to recognize that a certain symbol seems likely to appear when your pre-

Ancient Dream Journals

Dream journals are anything but a modern invention. The idea of them actually dates back to at least the fifth century, when Synesius of Cyrene wrote about "night books" in *On Dreams*. He also suggested the benefit of combining day journals with dream journals; in Section 12 of his tome, he notes: "We shall therefore see fit to add to what are called 'day books' what we term 'night books,' so as to have records to remind us of the character of each of the two lives concerned."

One You, One Journal

As you've likely noticed, some of the possible categories that you can include in your dream journal are related to things that occur during the day. If it aligns with your needs and feels like it would yield more connectivity and insights, consider having your day journal and your dream journal in one book.

slumber thoughts were centered on a certain subject. As such, its appearance in your dreams may then have you realize that it's serving as a beacon that's symbolizing something about this particular waking-life consideration. This then allows you to approach your dream decoding with fresh insights.

Through tracking themes, evening thoughts, and a recurring symbol, we can see patterns that may emerge. Through this, we can see patterns that may emerge. In this case, the presence of the crow more often than not relates to dream themes that have to do with movement and shifting elevations, as well as pre-sleep ruminations related to work. By knowing this, next time a crow appears, or we find ourselves moving from one level to another, we may look to our dream to see what it may be revealing about a work situation.

You could do this cross-referencing with any variables. For example, if you track themes and Moon phases, you may find that your dreams around the Full Moon are oftentimes more rife with conflict than those at other times of the month. Or, if you observe your feelings and your sleeping environment, you may potentially find a connection between the quality of slumber you had and the emotional tone infused in your dream. How to do this is easy: just create a log in your dream journal where you cross-reference different categories of dream information.

TABLE OF CONTENTS

Allocate several pages in the beginning of your dream journal to create a Table of Contents. It should include basic information, such as the date and title of each dream, as well as the page number. This will allow you to have an ongoing inventory of your dreams. Even just briefly scanning it will provide you with important insights based upon their titles.

Dreaming Rituals on the Road

As you're always dreaming, you can bring your intentional dreamwork practice with you wherever you go. Your portable dream kit may include your dream journal, dream pillow, and flower essences that aid your slumber. Bring them — especially your journal — along with you in your carry-on, as you never know what elevated visions you may have when at high elevations. Don't forget to pack the things that help you sleep well and have you feel at home wherever you are. If you're unsure about the light and noise environment of your hotel room, bring a sleep mask, earplugs, and/or a mini-pink noise machine with you. You can also still enjoy your favorite centering essential oils on the road: use a travel-size aromatherapy diffuser or pack a premade mist that you can spritz yourself with before sleeping. Also, a dream altar will travel: bring along crystals, candles, sacred images, etc., and create a mini-altar on your hotel nightstand.

Famous Dreamers' Diaries

Have you ever been intrigued about the dreams of famous people? If so, you can read the oneiric visions of some who have shared their dreams in published works, whether it be in books solely dedicated to the subject or included in ones on a broader concept. These include:

William S. Burroughs, *My Education: A Book of Dreams*

Graham Greene, *A World of My Own: A Dream Diary*

Henry Rollins, *61 Dreams* (part of *Black Coffee Blues*)

Federico Fellini, *The Book of Dreams*

Jack Kerouac, *Book of Dreams*

Vladimir Nabokov, *Insomniac Dreams*

Other Pages to Include in Your Dream Journal

Here are two other categories that you can include in your dream journal.

Dream Themes

Create a page in your journal where you catalog a list of themes, images, people, and places that commonly appear in your dreams. This way, if you're struggling to remember a dream one morning, you can glance at the theme page to see if it will shake your memory, helping you recall some of the who, what, and where that wove through your dream.

Dream Signs

If you do lucid dreaming, identifying dream signs can be essential in helping you become conscious that you're in a dream. To enhance your facility with recognizing them, it's good to have a list of the places, events, people, or perspectives that commonly appear in your dreams but never occur in your waking life. Go through your journal to find these, and then dedicate a page to a creating a dream-sign list that you can have for handy reference. Review it before you go to sleep, so that you can prime your mind to recognize these when you're in a dream, as this can help to activate your lucidity ability.

CHAPTER NINE

DECODING YOUR DREAMS

As you've likely experienced, the process of recalling, recording, and journaling your dreams itself can help to lift the veil that may have obscured your understanding as to what meaning they carried. Additionally, there are other approaches that can further help us decipher their significance. Of course, while working with a trained psychotherapist or dreamworker can offer you a personalized way to render more clarity, there are other ways that you can decode your dreams on your own, or with a community of others also interested in illuminating the wisdom of their oneiric visions. In this chapter, we'll explore approaches that will further help us to understand our dreams. We'll survey dream dictionaries, a Jungian technique known as Active Imagination, and popular divining methods. We'll also consider ways to tap into the power that comes through banding together with others, including working with a dreamwork partner and becoming involved with a dream group.

Dream Dictionaries and Symbol Books

One of the ways that many people gain insights into their dreams is by consulting a dream dictionary. As shared in the Introduction, interpretations of dream symbols were included in cuneiform tablets of the Library of Ashurbaniplal, dating from the seventh century BCE. While it was Artemidorus who is credited with writing one of the first and most comprehensive dream guide books back in the second century CE, his is not necessarily the oldest. Generally, dream dictionaries are books — or online databases — that are arranged in an A to Z format. You use them to look up an image that appeared in your dream to find out what it's commonly thought to represent. As you look through the interpretations, you may become more clear as to the potential meaning that the dream symbol possibly holds for you.

However, while these guides may help to catalyze your ability to become more fluent with images and their range of significance, it's important to not just adopt a particular meaning that's in the book and definitively apply it to your dream. Rather, it's important to see whether any of the associated meanings intuitively resonate with you and feel personally relevant. After all, while there are aspects of symbols that are thought to be universal, what one signifies to you may be different than what it does for another person. Sages throughout time, including Artemidorus himself, believed that the meaning of oneiric images was personal to the dreamer.

If reading about the different meanings of images is helpful to you in understanding your oneiric visions, there are other books that you can consult in addition to traditional dream dictionaries. These include books that catalog symbols that have held meaning for cultures throughout history. With their glossary-like approach, they may be similar to dream dictionaries, but not named as such. Again, though, be cautious in taking what is written and applying it to your dream without running it through your inner sense of truth to determine its personal veracity.

Active Imagination

Among his other breakthrough theories and accomplishments, Carl Jung pioneered a technique called Active Imagination, which can be used to bring forth a deeper level of understanding as to the insights that our dreams are dispatching. Active Imagination is a process by which you marry your conscious and unconscious minds to bring forth awareness and healing. And while it can be used as a general meditative and illuminative technique, it can also play a key role in helping us give voice to the wisdom that is carried forth by dream images and characters. When you use Active Imagination with your dreams, you begin by first finding yourself in a tranquil and reflective state. You invite in the recollections of a current dream, with the intention of having a dialogue with a character or symbol that it featured.

Once one of them emerges in your mind, you begin to converse with it. The trick is that you don't forcibly create the questions or answers, but rather allow them to arise, seeing what is stirred up and inspired by your imaginal mind. You beckon the dream image or character to provide you with clarification, asking them what they signified and what lessons they have for you. You can do Active Imagination quietly in your mind or in conversations out loud (and record them if you want). It can also be done with automatic writing, or through drawing, painting, music, or dance.

Doing Active Imagination with dreams can be quite an amazing process. You may find that it yields powerful surprises as you witness what spontaneously comes forth. After practicing it, especially with images or figures that have played a recurring starring role in your dreams, you may notice that they no longer appear with such frequency; the process of Active Imagination may allow you to get a direct line as to the communiqué they were carrying, making their role in your dreams no longer necessary. For many, it's best to start doing Active Imagination with someone trained in the method, such as a Jungian analyst or a professional schooled in the technique. Given that it gives your imaginal realm great freedom to express itself, it's thought that those who readily get lost in fantasy may want to exhibit caution in doing this practice, or only do it with a trained practitioner.

Tarot

If you work with tarot cards, you can turn to them to access more insights into what your dream may be revealing to you. If we think about how tarot cards are filled with images, reflect a visual landscape, and are embedded with archetypal symbols, it makes sense that they can help us garner more awareness as to what our dreams may be illuminating. Working with the tarot may aid you in accessing the part of your mind that is at home in this realm, acting as a conduit to help you better recall and understand your dreams.

There are several ways that you can work with the tarot to help decipher your dreams. One simple way is to think about a particular image that arose, about which you don't feel clear. Holding it in your mind's eye, pick a card and see what it reflects back to you. Another way is to do a tarot layout.

Deciphering Dreams with Tarot

To get more detailed insights into your dream, you can do a layout using three tarot cards. With this approach, it may be easier to work with the twenty-two cards of the Major Arcana, rather than the full deck.

1   Pick three cards, laying them down on a table in front of you from left to right.

2   Looking at the first card, consider that it represents the potential opportunity the dream (or a particular dream image) is pointing you toward. Reading about the card in a book, or looking to what you already know about it, see what it reflects to you about your dream.

3   Looking at the second card, consider that it represents a potential challenge about which the dream (or dream image) is making you aware. Reflect upon what this may signify.

4   Looking at the third card, consider that it is offering you guidance on how to orient to a situation in your life given what the first and second cards revealed. Reflect upon what this may signify.

If you have an ongoing tarot practice, you could also do more elaborate layouts — such as the Celtic Cross — using the whole deck to get even more detailed insights.

THE MAJOR ARCANA CARDS OF THE TAROT

While there are numerous tarot resources, both in print and online, for ready access, here is a list of the twenty-two Major Arcana cards, their associated number, and some keywords accorded with each.

0 – The Fool
Courage, innocence, freedom, risk-taking, rebellion, breakthroughs

1 – The Magician
Beginnings, learning, discipline, manifestation, intentions, communication

2 – The High Priestess
Intuition, reflection, contemplation, knowing, sacred knowledge, divine feminine

3 – The Empress
Love, pleasure, beauty, creativity, luxury, sensuality

4 – The Emperor
Authority, foundations, empowerment, responsibility, leadership, dignity

5 – The Hierophant
Tradition, community, faith, teacher, knowledge, sacred vows

6 – The Lovers
Discernment, choice, relationship crossroads, commitment, learning, wholeness

7 – The Chariot
Ambition, intuition, forward movement, self-realization, beginnings, integrity

8 – Strength
Patience, passion, self-love, gentleness, vulnerability, self-care

9 – The Hermit
Solitude, faith, inner journey, service, guidance, vigilance

10 – Wheel of Fortune
Change, opportunity, expansion, luck, new possibilities, flexibility

11 – Justice
Balance, harmony, adjustment, inner peace, truth, judgment

12 – The Hanged Man
Surrender, disillusionment, paradox, martyrdom, perspective, divinity

13 – Death
Endings, completion, transformation, liberation, internal change, regeneration

14 – Temperance
Art, learning, alchemy, creativity, integration, balance of opposites

15 – The Devil
Fear, obsession, control, power struggles, creativity, dark side

16 – The Tower
Fundamental change, destruction, chaos, dismantling, endings, healing

17 – The Star
Inspiration, destiny, imagination, dreams, creativity, future

18 – The Moon
Shadow, past, illusions, dreamscapes, deception, illumination

19 – The Sun
Freedom, innocence, new beginnings, enthusiasm, vitality, success

20 – Judgment
Accountability, reckoning, life review, truth, awakening, self-acceptance

21 – The World
Completion, empowerment, achievement, manifestation, big picture, leadership

Pendulum

Another way to gain insight into your dreams is by dowsing with a pendulum. The use of finding hidden information or items with this approach goes back thousands of years, with ancient Egyptian bas-reliefs showing people using these instruments. A pendulum is composed of a string, usually a light chain, that has a weighted stone or crystal attached to it. It's designed in such a way that when held, the crystal or stone is able to swing in an unobstructed manner.

You can use a pendulum to access answers to questions, with certain observed movements signifying a specific answer and others a different one; generally, when using a pendulum, most people assign a certain movement to accord to a Yes response, another to a No response, and another to reflect a response that indicates uncertainty. People use pendulums for insights on a variety of subjects, including to probe more deeply into what their dreams may have signified.

Using a Pendulum

If you're not clear about what a dream symbol means, you can see what insights you can access using the pendulum. Here's a simple way to do it:

1 Look in a dream dictionary or symbol book for all the meanings associated with the image in which you're interested in decoding.

2 Focusing upon one meaning at a time, as you're holding the pendulum, pose the question, "Is this what the dream image signifies for me?"

3 As you go through each possible meaning, see for which one/s the pendulum's movement yields an affirmative answer. This may help you refine your understanding as to the significance that your dream symbol contained.

The *I Ching*

The *I Ching* is a time-honored book that offers a wellspring of wisdom from Taoism and Confucianism. It features an oracular method to tap into prized philosophical knowledge, including to access more insights into your dreams. For over three thousand years, it's been used to provide guidance and counsel to people from all swaths of life, from kings to commoners. The *I Ching* is also known as *The Book of Changes*. It contains sixty-four hexagram designs, each of which has a name and number, and is associated with a trove of

EXERCISE

Working with the I Ching

1 Focus on a question that you have about an aspect of your dream or its meaning in toto.

2 As you are doing this, toss your divination objects — whether yarrow sticks, coins, or specialized dice — onto a surface in front of you.

3 Consulting an *I Ching* book, determine which hexagram is mirrored by the result of your toss.

4 Read the resultant hexagram through the lens of answering your dream-meaning inquiry.

time-honored wisdom. To "consult the *I Ching*" — and discover the hexagram that mirrors your inquiry — you use a technique that involves throwing either yarrow sticks, coins, or specialized dice, and doing a calculation based upon what results.

Dreamwork Partners

One way to further understand what your dreams may be revealing is to work with a dreamwork partner. This would be someone that you trust, perhaps a relied-upon friend or colleague, who is also interested in dreamwork. They would need to be someone with whom you feel comfortable sharing the intimacies of your inner self, as revealed by what comes forth in your dreams.

Working with a dreamwork partner can not only help you to access deeper awareness as to what your dreams signify, but it will also assist you to more readily remember your dreams. After all, if you're committing to another person that you will be capturing and recounting your dreams, you will be motivated to do so. Doing dreamwork with a partner is a powerful way to not only dive deeper into your dreams, but it can help you to establish the strong relationship bond that comes from honestly sharing yourself with another person. Once you and your partner have decided that you would like to support each other in your dreamwork, set a few guidelines for engagement. Here are several steps to follow that will help you create a partnership that will be rewarding.

MAKE A TIME COMMITMENT

Decide upon a time frame, perhaps a month or two, to which you will commit to being dreamwork partners, after which time you can reevaluate how the process is serving you both. Knowing that your commitment is bounded and won't go on for an undetermined time, it will help each of you be more steadfast in your allegiance to the process.

DETERMINE YOUR SHARING FREQUENCY

Choose a consistent frequency with which to share your dreams with each other. Generally, anywhere from daily to weekly works best. If you're only sharing select dreams, you could even extend it to every other week. Beyond that, too much time passes, and the strength of the work seems to dissipate.

WAYS TO SHARE YOUR DREAMS

Determine how you want to share your dreams. Will you do so via email or video chat, on the phone or in person? You may also decide that you want to do some sort of hybrid approach if that works better for you. For some people, just having another person hear their dreams provides enough value. It enables them to feel witnessed, and the accountability of having to share dreams on a regular basis motivates them to focus on recording them. For others, however, the richness of the experience comes through getting their partner's reflections on their dreams, as that serves as a vehicle to help further discover their meanings.

HOW TO OFFER REFLECTIONS

If you decide to offer reflections upon each other's dreams, decide what type and how much you want. Is a sentence or two adequate, or do you both want what you receive to be more in-depth if the dream warrants it? Will you offer your thoughts on all the dreams that you each send to the other, or only on a select number? If the latter, decide who — the dreamer or their partner — gets to determine which dreams will get more in-depth treatment. Again, having these clear expectations as to what you give and what you receive does wonders for the relationship and the communication that it entails.

When giving reflection, it's a good practice to start with "If this were my dream ..." It creates a boundary and clarifies that each of you is offering your personal associations, rather than stating an objective analysis of the dream. It reminds each person that it is truly the dreamer who has ownership over the dream, and, as such, is the one who knows what it really signifies. The other person is just offering perspectives that may help the dreamer realize what that significance is.

Dream Groups

While working with a dreamwork partner can help you access insights that may not otherwise be available, so can being part of a dream group. Also referred to as dream clubs, they offer a collective approach to mining the messages that may be carried in our dreams. One of the pioneers of the dream group model was Montague Ullman, MD (who, you may remember from chapter 2, was also a trailblazer in researching precognitive and telepathic dreams). What follows is a process you can use to coordinate a dream group meeting, which reflects many of the tenets that Ullman designed and tested over the years. The benefits of this approach are multi-fold, including having a group of people hold space for someone to share a dream elevates its significance. And, committing to an ongoing dreamwork practice can enhance participants' dream recall. Additionally, having numerous people offer their vantage points helps to further reveal the essence of the dreams shared. Plus, being part of a dream group can be a fun activity as it brings you together in a newly forged community, enjoying all the advantages that this yields.

Dream groups may be led by psychotherapists or dreamworkers, although just as likely they may be a group of laypersons who come together to share their collective interest. They may be in-person groups or those that meet online. If you can't find one, or don't align with any that exist, consider starting one. Put out an invitation to friends and colleagues who may be interested. You want the group to be small enough so that everyone can share, but large enough so that there is adequate heterogeneity and fodder for conversation. Many suggest that six to eight people is a good size.

Dream groups often meet weekly or biweekly. In the beginning, you may want to define a finite time frame for the group, perhaps getting everyone to commit to several months. After that, you can then reassess whether to extend it. And while the members may change, many dream groups find that they go on for years. To create a safe and reliable container for the dream group, it's good to have a few guidelines in place. These can include:

- Group members should speak about dreams with reverent appreciation and maintain a strong respect for one another.

- The group should adopt a stance of confidentiality. Nothing that is shared within the group should be discussed with anyone outside of it, and no recording should be allowed unless everyone in the group agrees. The exception to this could be that each member can share a dream of theirs that the group workshopped — and what they learned — with a friend or their therapist, but it should be done in a manner that safeguards the other members' privacy.

- Everyone should remember that the person who shares their dream is the ultimate authority on it. While others play an active role in its deciphering by giving reflection and asking questions that help the interpretation to unfold, ultimately it's the dreamer who knows the meaning it holds for them. The group just helps them discover it, acting as sherpas, supporting them on the journey to clarify the gift that it offers.

- The person who shares their dream gets to be in charge of declaring when they feel that the process of inquiry is complete for them, calling for the end of it. Even if others still believe there is more matter to be mined, the dreamer has the ultimate say on when they feel complete.

- Someone should assume the role of being the group leader. If it works for the group dynamic, you can change who assumes this role in subsequent gatherings. The leader shepherds the movement between the different stages of the process and keeps the conversation flowing.

STAGE 1: THE DREAMER SHARES

One person (or two, depending upon time) elects to share a dream that they found to be interesting, curious, and/or meaningful. It should be a dream that is recent enough so that they can remember its details, as well as what was transpiring in their life around the time that they had it. That said, if a group member has a dream from years ago that's stayed with them, and which they regard as important and impactful, they can share it. They should communicate as much of the dream as they remember and as much as they feel comfortable sharing. They should recount it without any editing or commentary, either about the dream or their waking life. It's important that they don't share any potential analysis, as they don't want to bias the group as to what their interpretation will be.

The group should listen intently and take notes if they desire. Some groups like to have the dreamer type up the dream, read it aloud, and then share a copy with everyone. This can be helpful in capturing details that may be otherwise missed while listening to the dream's retelling. After the dreamer shares their dream, members of the group can ask questions if they need clarification. These questions should be focused on the content of the dream, not what it may mean.

STAGE 2: THE GROUP MEMBERS SHARE

Next, the group members mirror back reflections to the dreamer. They share how the dream made them feel, what was stirred for them while listening to it. They should work with the images, seeing what arises for them in terms of metaphorical meanings. This can be done in a certain order; for example, by going around in a circle. Or the group members can share in a more spontaneous fashion.

As previously noted in the dreamwork partner section, it's always important for someone who is witnessing another's dream to have their reflections begin with the statement, "If this were my dream…" This helps to remind everyone that the only person who truly knows what the dream signifies is the person to whom it belongs, allowing them to maintain ownership of it. Members share reflections until the process feels complete; this is something that the leader can help distinguish.

If it feels right, someone can write down the group's reflections on a blackboard, whiteboard, or large notepad on an easel. This can be helpful, since it's often a good idea to synthesize what the group had shared before this step is complete. During this whole process, the dreamer remains silent, attentively listening.

STAGE 3: THE DREAMER AND THE GROUP DIALOGUE

In this stage, the dreamer notes which group members' reflections most notably resonated with them, and which ones didn't. To get deeper into the potential that this stage holds, the group can ask further questions of the dreamer: about their experience of the dream and how they feel it may relate to situations in their current life.

If a group member perceives that the dreamer isn't readily making connections between the dream and situations that are unfolding in their life, they can gently and compassionately nudge them by asking about what occurred the day before the dream. They can even inquire as to what they were thinking about before they went to bed. Yet, they shouldn't push the dreamer to make realizations that they are not ready to.

At some point, it becomes apparent when the process is finished and all that is to be evidenced has been brought forth. At this point, the leader can ask the group member who shared their dream if they feel that the group work is complete. If the dreamer has typed up and shared their dream, someone can read it aloud at the end, marking the closure of the process.

CHAPTER TEN

ASTRODREAMWORK

If you're looking for another way to work with your oneiric visions, consider using an astrological approach to dreaming, a method I call AstroDreamwork. Given that both dreams and astrology are vehicles for self-awareness, they can work together to synergistically help us access an even deeper level of understanding. As you'll see, astrology can aid us in accessing and translating the meaning of our dreams, while dreams give us insights that can further reveal the fount of self-knowledge potentiated within our astrology charts and the current zeitgeist through which we are living. Even if you don't know much about astrology, you may find that AstroDreamwork offers you supernal benefits.

A Traditional Practice

Astrology is a sacred art that has guided cultures throughout history. With roots dating back to Babylonia in the second millennium BCE, astrology has been used for providing counsel and guidance ever since. While it previously was the provenance of priests, physicians, and court advisors, in the twentieth century, it became ever more accessible to laypersons with the publication of the first horoscope columns. Today, as we continue to seek self-knowledge as well as glean answers to larger universal questions, astrology has made further inroads into popular culture.

The connection between astrology and dreams has roots at least as far back as medieval times. It was during this period that court astrologers would serve as counsel for kings, providing them with divinatory insights that would guide their approach to affairs of state, including when to arrange meetings or whether to proceed with battles. Some of these prized insights would come through interpreting the dreams of the nobility, as their oneiric visions were viewed as being divinely informed.

Astrologers today who practice medieval-astrology techniques use these classic principles when working with the dreams of their clients. Some of the notable texts that feature guidelines for this practice include *The Book of Astronomy* by Guido Bonatti, who, in the thirteenth century, served as advisor to numerous leaders, including Holy Roman Emperor Frederick II. Another classic tome is the *Complete Book on the Judgment of the Stars* by Ali Ibn Abi al-Rijal, written in the eleventh century and translated into Latin four centuries later.

Using these techniques, astrologers create charts for the moment a client asks them a question about a dream they've had. From there, they use methods to first assess whether the dream has value in understanding a pressing situation. If the dream is found to hold insights, the astrologer then looks to the planets in certain areas of the astrology chart to try to understand the nature of the dream. They then do further analysis to see if and how what occurred in the dream is likely to manifest in waking life, partially assessed by looking at key features of the Moon in the astrology chart. While this particular approach takes skill and experience, you need not be a practicing astrologer to be able to turn to astrology to access more awareness about your dreams. Following are numerous ways in which you can practice AstroDreamwork.

Your Signs, Your Dreams

Your personal astrology chart holds the keys to understanding the unique signatures that make you who you are. Your astrology chart can help you decipher what your dreams are revealing, while your dreams can unlock the mysteries of your astrology chart. And while astrologers who practice AstroDreamwork may minister to their client's dreams through the lens of their full natal chart, even a cursory understanding of your personal astrology can give you stellar insights into deciphering your dreams. You only need to look to your Sun sign (what you answer when someone asks you, "What's your sign?"), and if you know them, your Moon and Ascendant signs as well. As zodiacal signs express who we are, their characteristics are those that we tap into during our waking life. Knowing about our signs, we can see why it may be that we act a certain way, ruminate about a particular topic, approach situations through a particular emotional vantage point, or find ourselves motivated toward certain activities. These are facets of ourselves that also show up in our dreams.

Since the sign that our Sun is in — as well as the ones that our Moon and Ascendant are in — represent core principles of who we are, we may find that their associated signatures appear in our dreams with some regularity. After all, they are reflections of the archetypes with which we are connected, and how we express much of who we are, whether in our waking life or our dreaming life.

EXERCISE

A Stellar Approach to Dreams

Here's a simple AstroDreamwork approach you can try.

- Since most people know their Sun sign, first read the keywords associated with yours. Remember that the Sun represents your vitality, identity, and the things that have you shine. And so, if you notice a dream that is filled with many of these themes and symbols, it may be that you're working through issues related to further expressing your identity and what it is that truly makes you tick.

- Now look to your Moon sign. Because the Moon represents what we find nourishing, as well as our unconscious instincts, the sign that it is in gives us distinct insights into what our dreams may be revealing about how we orient emotionally. If archetypes related to your Moon sign are quite present in a dream, it may be that you're trying to work out some powerful emotional issues and/or gain insights into how you can take better care of yourself.

- After that, look to your Ascendant sign (also known as the Rising sign), which signals how we present ourselves and move through the world. It also represents how we perceive the external world and orient to it. As our dreams reflect the way that we navigate through life, their backdrops may be infused with telltale images associated with our Ascendant sign. If your dream is particularly flush with concepts related to it, it may be that you're trying to solve challenges related to how to maneuver a current situation and/or you're reconsidering the way you want to present your image to the world.

THE ZODIAC SIGNS

Aries
Desire nature. Fast movements.
Battle of wills. Sharp objects. Impatience.
Warriors. Swords. Guns. Head. Rams.

Taurus
Sensual delights. Practical solutions.
Slow movements. Resistance to change.
Luxury items. Verdant scenery. Flowers.
Routines. Neck. Bulls.

Gemini
Dual approaches. Gathering information.
Need for variety. Intellectual orientation.
Schoolrooms. Breathing. Libraries.
Messengers. Arms. Twins.

Cancer
Family orientation. Maternal instincts.
Feeding people. Indirect movements.
Containers of safety. Kitchens. Gardens.
Moon. Stomach. Crabs.

Leo
Artistic expressions. Dramatic
performances. Romantic love. Pride.
Sun. Royalty. Gold. Children. Heart.
Lions.

Virgo
Filing systems. Fitness studios. Digestion.
Perfectionism. Crafts. Organization.
Details. Agriculture. Pets. Maidens.

Libra
Art galleries. Social gatherings.
Courtrooms. Equality. Indecision.
Diplomacy. Partnerships. Roses.
Skin. Scales.

Scorpio
Buried treasures. Deep emotions. Secrets.
Darkness. Transformation. Passion. Money.
Toilets. Genitals. Scorpions.

Sagittarius
Foreign lands. Religious sites. Big picture.
Truth. Philosophy. Adventures. Travel.
Liver. Archery. Horses.

Capricorn
Skeletal system. Old age. Time. Success.
Blueprints. Endurance. Delays. Knees.
Mountains. Goats.

Aquarius
Futuristic visions. Technological
advances. Humanitarian missions. Gadgets.
Innovation. Rebellions. Spaceships. Ankles.
Urns. Stars.

Pisces
Unconditional love. Blurred boundaries.
Mystical pursuits. Oceans. Sacrifices.
Compassion. Fog. Magic. Feet. Fish.

Dreams and the Moon

Throughout time, the Moon has represented our emotional nature, the sea of feelings in which we swim, and the tides of our personal unconscious. As such, it also is an archetypal symbol that represents our dreams. There are numerous ways that you can turn to the Moon when working with your oneiric visions.

THE LUNAR CYCLE

Throughout the month, the Moon moves through a cycle in which it appears to grow with light, reaching the culmination of a Full Moon. It then proceeds to have its illumination wane, receding back to darkness, before it again becomes a New Moon. The monthly New Moon is said to be a time in which we can initiate new beginnings. Several days before this new lunar cycle begins, the Moon holds and projects less and less — and finally an absence — of the Sun's rays. Referred to as the Balsamic Moon, this is the

The Four Elements

Zodiacal signs are often grouped together based upon the element to which they belong. Here are some qualities and symbols associated with each. You may be able to get more insights into what your dream symbols are revealing by looking to see if those associated with the elements of your Sun, Moon, and Ascendant appear with frequency in your dreams.

Fire (Aries, Leo, Sagittarius)
Flames, spirited action, candles, vertical movements, red, orange

Earth (Taurus, Virgo, Capricorn)
The earth, practical matters, physical structures, sensual experiences, green, brown

Air (Gemini, Libra, Aquarius)
Communication, conversations, balloons, wind, horizontal movement, yellow

Water (Cancer, Scorpio, Pisces)
Water, the sea, faucets, boats, aquatic creatures, blue

phase of the lunar cycle in which we're oriented to letting go and finding direction through connecting to the depth of illumination within ourselves; it's a time to be still, meditative, and reflective, seeing what arises from the depths of our intuition. As such, it's also an especially gorgeous time to tune in to what's being revealed through our dreams.

Many people like to make New Moon intentions, planting seeds for what they want to usher in during the month-long lunar cycle. By doing dream incubation in the last days of the Balsamic Moon and first days of the New Moon phases, we can gain further clarity as to what we may want to hone our focus upon to manifest over the coming four weeks. Before going to bed, ask that your dreams contain directionality as to what is ripe for growth in the ensuing month. You could pose this as a general inquiry, asking yourself something like, "Dreams, please point me to an understanding of what intention I should make for this new month."

Or, if you want to further target this practice, you can work with the energy of the sign in which the New Moon will appear. For example, for the New Moon that occurs during Capricorn season (the third week of December to the third week of January), you could ask your dreams to share insights with you into objectives you can undertake related to how to be more productive or efficient. Or, during the New Moon that takes place during Leo season (the third week of July through the third week of August), you could request clues as to how to bring more joy and creativity into your life. Look to page 112 to gain more insights into what each of the signs represents and therefore what a focused New Moon dream practice could target. Additionally, if you know your birth chart, you can get more details into what each New Moon is inspiring for you personally. For example, if it connects with your Venus, the following weeks may bring lessons in love, while if it takes up residency in the 11th House of your astrology chart, the coming month may hold opportunities for community work. Knowing this, you can then refine your dream-incubation inquiry.

Full Moon Dreams

The days around the monthly Full Moon seem as if they are filled with heightened energy. While some people find that they are more likely to have disrupted sleep during this period, others note that their dreams are more vivid and active around the time of the Full Moon. Be aware of any sleep and dream patterns that arise for you during this lunation.

1 Pay attention each month to when the Full Moon occurs.

2 Keep track of it in your dream journal, making a notation on the days that it takes place.

3 See whether the dreams you have around the Full Moon have a different level of intensity or feature certain themes. Note whether your sleeping pattern has a unique quality during this time of the month.

4 After a few months of tracking this, look through your dream journal to see if you can identify any patterns that connect your Full Moon dreams.

ECLIPSES

Each year, between four and seven eclipses occur. Some accord with New Moons (solar eclipses) and some with Full Moons (lunar eclipses). Even if we can't see an eclipse in the sky where we live, these celestial events are thought to coincide with powerful, life-changing events and reflections. Mark the eclipses on your calendar, and then see if your dreams have a different tone or yield unique perspectives the week before and after them. Once again, if you know your birth chart, you may be able to generate additional insights, since you will know which realms of your life the eclipses are highlighting.

Mercury, Venus, and Mars Retrograde

When it comes to astrological awareness, one of the phenomena that continues to capture many people's attention is Mercury Retrograde. As it turns out, the retrograde cycle of this quicksilver messenger planet — plus those of Venus and Mars — can be a time when doing AstroDreamwork can be very fruitful. To understand why, let's start with defining what it means when a planet is in its retrograde cycle. When this occurs, the planet appears — from our vantage point on Earth — to be moving backward in the sky, in motion apparently distinct from that of other celestial bodies. And while the perceived shift is an illusion caused by the paced pathways in which the different planets, including the Earth, orbit the Sun, astrologically, the retrograde cycle of planets is accorded with special meaning.

As the planets revisit territory already traveled during their retrograde phase, we are encouraged to do the same, going back to the past with fresh eyes. Our waking thoughts may feature our retracing of situations that we've already traversed...and so may what arises in our dreams. During these planetary retrogrades, you may notice more emphasis on people, places, situations, objects, and ideas from the past in your dreams. And as we reencounter previously traveled landscapes, we may see how our dreams are helping us to craft understanding in our present, based upon further acceptance and awareness of what came before, so that we can move forward with more clarity. And while, from our perspective on Earth, all planets experience a retrograde cycle, those of the trio known as the personal planets — Mercury, Venus, and Mars — seem to be a time when we access insights that inform us on a more individual level. As such, they serve as a stellar focus for AstroDreamwork.

MERCURY RETROGRADE

Mercury is the planet of communication. During its thrice-yearly retrograde cycle, we revisit ideas from the past in order to gain a new perspective, one that can bolster our ability to more clearly share thoughts and move about in the world. To this aim, during its retrograde cycle, symbols of Mercury — such as books, mail, cars, bicycles, planes, computers, and bridges — may populate our dreams. See what they are reflecting to you about learning and communicating from a different angle.

VENUS RETROGRADE

Venus Retrograde occurs every eighteen months, and is a time period in which we reevaluate what we value. During it, we may also find ourselves reconsidering our relationship realm and our approach to partnerships. In the course of its retrograde, symbols of Venus — such as luxury items, money, mirrors, lovers, objects of beauty, cosmetics, and artwork — may appear in our dreams. See how they point you toward further understanding the ways in which you can infuse your life with more worth and richness.

MARS RETROGRADE

Occurring every two-plus years, Mars Retrograde is a stretch of time during which we may find ourselves further understanding just what it is that we desire, as well as how we design the strategies with which we pursue what we covet. It's also a time to gather more understanding about our relationship with anger and frustration. During Mars Retrograde, symbols of this planet — such as swords, knives, fire, battles, warriors, athletes, sexual pursuits, and the color red — may appear more frequently in our dreams. See how they may aim your attention toward the ways in which you're reconsidering how you cultivate and direct your energy and will.

Remember to pay special attention to images or scenes that involve reflections of the past during all the retrograde cycles. Also note that it's often the days around the beginning and ending of these periods in which the themes associated with these planets, and the awareness we're encouraged to discover, may be more concentrated. Consider paying special attention to your dreams during these nights.

CHAPTER ELEVEN

NATURAL REMEDIES FOR DREAMING

Flower essences and crystals may help further connect to our dreams. In this chapter, you'll also learn all about herbal dream pillows, including how to make your own.

Flower Essences

There are numerous ways in which flower essences can help to inspire our dreamwork.

Angelica

Angelica helps us to feel wrapped in protection in the liminal space of our dreams, more open to the spiritual guidance that can come forth. And with that, it may inspire a deeper experience of connection, attunement, and remembrance within our oneiric visions.

Cosmos

There are times when we can "see" our dreams upon waking, but it's hard to access them in a way that allows us to communicate them in words. Cosmos flower essence helps to bridge the third-eye and throat chakras, which may assist us in giving voice to our dreams and documenting them more readily.

Iris

If your dreams feel lifeless and less than animated, consider Iris flower essence. It is thought to add color, both literally and figuratively, to our visions, helping us to rekindle the creative inspiration that dreams can offer us.

Morning Glory

If you wake up with a dulled and drowsy feeling, as if part of you hasn't returned from your dreamscape, Morning Glory may be a great flower essence to use. It can help us ground back in our bodies and be more in sync with rhythms of light and dark, awake and sleep.

Mugwort

Mugwort is a plant traditionally associated with dreaming. In its flower essence form, it's said to stimulate the psyche's receptive capacity for awareness during our oneiric journeys. Additionally, it may help us to be better able to bridge awareness between dreams and waking life, enhancing the integrated weaving of insights experienced in each into the other.

Shasta Daisy

Sometimes we can understand parts of our dream, but we're unclear as to how they all weave together. To help forge a clearer vision as to the broader meaning of a dream and how all the pieces may thread together as a whole, try Shasta Daisy flower essence.

St. John's Wort

St. John's Wort was traditionally heralded as the flower of protection. In its essence form, it's thought to offer protection to those who are psychically sensitive and feel undefended in their dreams. Therefore, it may be a helpful remedy for people who experience nightmares.

Star Tulip

Star Tulip is a wonderful essence to help augment inner listening and receptivity. That makes it great for use in activities, such as dreaming, in which we want assistance tuning in to the awareness that's streaming forth from the depths of our minds.

Crystals

Many people like to incorporate crystals and gemstones into their self-care regimens, including using them for enhancing sleep and dreams. They are so beautiful that even those who don't accord them with wisdom significance find that there's something so alluring about them: the way they capture and reflect light, the dance of colors in which they are imbued, and the energy — sometimes subtle and sometimes powerful — that they emit. And that's not even considering the awe that arises when you stop to think how they are the result of thousands and thousands of years of geological transformation, fostering a feeling of connection to the Earth and a sense of timelessness.

And while some think of them as a new-age fad, the power accorded to them cuts across time and culture. It's been noted that the ancient Egyptians buried their dead with crystals, as they were thought to protect them in their journey to the afterlife. It's said that the first-century CE Roman general Plautius instructed his soldiers to cover themselves with hematite, found in the soil upon which they were fighting; it was thought that doing so would bestow upon them protection from Mars, the god of war, during the battles in which they were engaged. And let's not forget that in the *Vedas*, the classic Indian texts, there includes numerous mentions of the remedial effects of gemstones. Additionally, modern-day discoveries have found that some gemstones carry important properties. For example, certain quartz crystals have piezoelectricity, generating electrical potential when mechanical stress is applied to them.

CHOOSING DREAMWORK CRYSTALS

There are hundreds, if not thousands, of different types of crystals and gemstones; how do you choose which ones to weave into your dreamwork? Here are three different approaches that you can use.

1. Crystal Nature

The first approach is to explore crystals that have been noted to have properties that benefit different aspects of dreamwork. These include:

- **Enhance Dream Recall**: Celestite, Kyanite
- **Encourage Lucid Dreaming**: Danburite, Pink Moonstone

Working with Crystals

There are numerous ways that you can work with crystals to inspire your dreams. Some ideas include:

- Use them as a talisman, placing them under your pillow, on your nightstand, or on your dream altar. Just knowing that your intentionally chosen gemstones are within view may help amplify your dream connection.

- Lay out gemstones in a crystal grid to give more power to your dream intentions. You can find details on how to do this in books and online.

- Crystal-grid your bedroom. For example, you could place a special crystal in each corner of the room. After doing so, use a wand-shaped crystal to connect the energetic matrix. Doing this could both amplify the energy of your bedroom sanctuary and make it feel more like a protected space.

- As you incorporate crystals into your dreamwork practice, tune in to see what, if any, shifts emerge over the coming week or so. Do certain colors appear in your dreams? Specific themes? Particular feeling tones? Note this in your dream journal so that you can assess the effects of this practice.

121

Crystals and Dream Incubation

Here are two ways to work with crystals and dream-incubation practice. One simple way is to just hold your gemstone in your hand as you focus in on your incubation intention. Before you drift off to sleep, place it under your pillow, or on your nightstand. As you wake up, once again hold your crystal in your hand and see if it helps you further remember what came forth in your dream. Another technique is to have your crystal grid be focused upon your dream-incubation intention. Write down your intention on a piece of paper, fold it, and place that in the center of your crystal mandala. Design your grid around your intention, choosing a layout shape (i.e., spiral, infinity loop, etc.) that resonates with you, placing crystals in the various spots. Finally, place a center crystal on top of your written intention. Using a crystal wand, trace all of the crystals to unite them vibrationally. As you go to sleep, focus upon what insights you want your dream to reveal, holding the image of your crystal grid in your mind's eye.

- *Foster Understanding of a Dream's Meaning:* Amethyst, Selenite
- *Promote Dreams of Insight:* Jade, Moonstone
- *Help Protect Against Nightmares:* Pink Calcite, Smoky Quartz

2. Crystal Themes

In the second method, you choose crystals that are focused upon the themes that you're finding yourself to be working through in your dreams. While a crystal dictionary can help you find those supportive of an array of aims, here are a few examples to consider.

- *Bolstered Self-Esteem:* Citrine, Chrysoberyl
- *Enhanced Creativity:* Carnelian, Turquoise
- *Greater Self-Love and Compassion:* Rose Quartz, Rhodochrosite
- *Healing from Addictions:* Amethyst, Iolite
- *Working Through Relationship Challenges:* Dioptase, Lapis Lazuli

3. Crystal Curiosity

The third way to decide upon crystals to use in dreamwork is to be led by your intentional curiosity. Visit a gemstone store and see which ones call to you. Focus upon the benefit that you'd like the crystal to provide, whether that's helping you better remember your dreams, access more lucidity, feel more protected should you have a nightmare, or any of your other oneiric aims. Based upon this, see which ones you are magnetized toward.

Herbal Dream Pillows

Teas made from herbs have slumber-inspiring properties. Another way that you can use herbs and botanicals to support your sleep and dreams is by making a dream pillow. Also referred to as comfort pillows or dreamtime pillows, they have been used for centuries as part of nighttime rituals. One of the first recipes for dream pillows was included in the 1606 book *Ram's Little Dodeon: A Brief Epitome of the New Herbal, or History of Plants* by William Ram. It featured rose petals combined with mint powder and clove powder. Both King George III and Abraham Lincoln are said to be among those who used a pillow filled with hops to help them sleep.

How may they work? Fragrances connect to the brain's limbic system and help encourage different feeling states, including pacificity and relaxation. As such, the subtle scents emitted from a dream sachet tucked underneath your pillow, or placed on your nightstand, can help lull you to sleep and to dream. Their effects, though, may not cease once slumber falls upon you. After all, our brains are thought to process smells when we sleep, with researchers suggesting that fragrance experienced while dozing may impact the emotional currents of our dreams.

While premade dream pillows are available, it's also easy to make your own. It could be a fun and creative project to do solo or with friends or family. Also consider it as another DIY activity that you could do with your children or grandchildren if you're looking for an additional way to help them forge a connection with their dreams. (See the next page for tips on making your own herbal dream pillow.)

How to Make a Dream Pillow

A dream pillow consists of two parts: the covering, and the herbs that will fill it.

The Covering

You could go a very simple route and choose to use premade small cotton muslin bags with drawstrings. The advantage to this approach is that it cuts down on preparation time. The drawback is that it may not be as pretty and personalized. Or you could make your own pillow covering. To do so:

124

1. Buy natural fiber fabric such as cotton, linen, or silk. Wash it before creating your pillow covering so that any dyes or odors can be released.

2. Determine the size you want your finished pillow to be and cut it about ¾ to 1 inch (2 to 2.5 cm) bigger on all sides to allow for sewn seams. Some people prefer square ones while others like them rectangular. The only real confine you have is that it fits neatly under your pillow. If you like more fragrance, then use a larger size; if you'd rather it be subtler, opt for a smaller one.

3 Fold your fabric with the right sides facing each other. Sew it on the two sides perpendicular to the fold, as well as one-quarter of the way in on either side on the part that opposes the fold. Just make sure you leave enough room to put the herbs and flowers in.

4 Turn the pillowcase through the opening so that it is right side out.

5 Fill it with the herbs and flowers of your choice; you can either put them in loose or place them in a smaller muslin bag, and then fill the rest of the pillow with stuffing material.

6 Stitch up the opening. You can either do the whole project with a sewing machine or sew it by hand. If you'd rather not sew, you can always use seam tape, which just needs to be ironed to create closure.

The Herbs

There are numerous dried herbs and flowers you can use to fill your dream pillow. While the following are some of those traditionally used, if you have a favorite whose scent brings you joy, don't hesitate to include it. Just remember to briefly rub the dream pillow when you get into bed, as this will help to release its natural fragrances.

Lavender | With its sweetly floral scent, lavender is one of the premier flowers associated with calm and relaxation. Research has found that it helps increase levels of melatonin, the hormone necessary for good sleep. It also seems to have memory-boosting qualities, with one study suggesting that one of its chief constituents (linalool) could reduce the cognitive impairment that occurs with REM deprivation.

Mugwort | The Greek goddess Artemis, from which mugwort gets its botanical name (*Artemisia douglasiana*), was a Moon deity. When we remember that the Moon, archetypally, is associated with sleep and dreams, it's no coincidence that this is one of the herbs prized by a multitude of societies for its ability to herald vivid and prophetic dreams. Many native tribes, including the Paiute and Chumash (the latter who refer to mugwort as "dream sage"), use it to promote sacred dreaming.

Rose Petals | Take inspiration from *Ram's Little Dodeon* and include rose petals in your dream sachet. The fragrance of rose is thought to be calming and reduce anxiety. Plus, it infuses one with a sense of romanticism and love, thoughts of which are lovely to fall asleep to, and which may inspire heart-opening dreamscapes.

Rosemary | Greek scholars wore wreathes of rosemary to abet their studying, as it was prized for aiding concentration and fortifying memory, qualities supported by many research studies. And while it brightens the mind, it does so while promoting relaxation. This makes it a great fragrance for not only galvanizing dreams, but also helping you remember them in the morning.

Yarrow | Yarrow flowers, with their fresh and herbaceous scent, can make a beautiful addition to a dream sachet. One of yarrow's reputed properties — its ability to energetically create a sheath of protection — is a plus for those who want to feel shielded during sleep. Plus, yarrow may also bring visions of love; in times past, young women would place yarrow beneath their pillow and say a little prayer in hopes of meeting their future husband in their dream.

Others | Hops are among the most traditionally used herbs for promoting sleep. Roman chamomile is relaxing and thought to protect against nightmares in folk medicine. Lemon balm is known for its calming properties. Orris root is added to dream pillows to extend the fragrance of the other flowers and herbs.

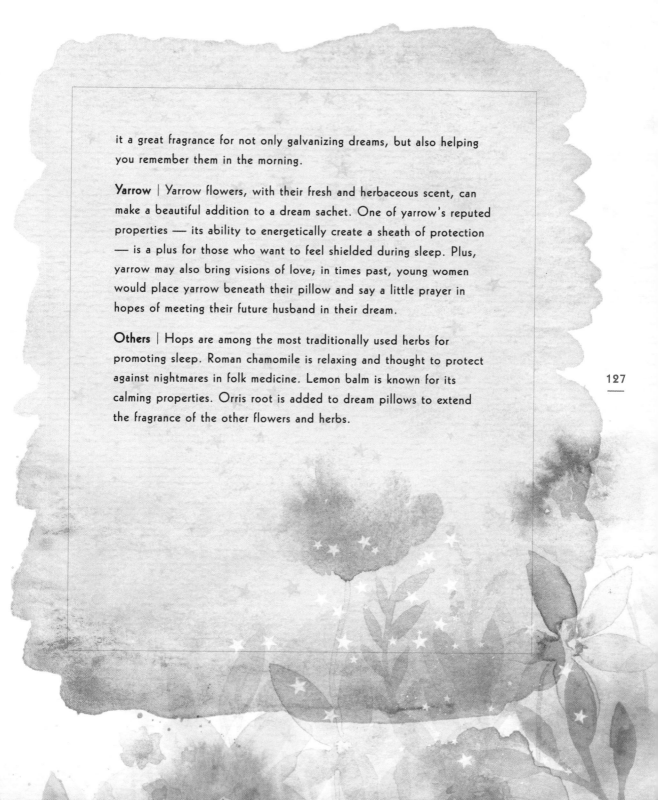

Brimming with creative inspiration, how-to projects, and useful information to enrich your everyday life, Quarto Knows is a favorite destination for those pursuing their interests and passions. Visit our site and dig deeper with our books into your area of interest: Quarto Creates, Quarto Cooks, Quarto Homes, Quarto Lives, Quarto Drives, Quarto Explores, Quarto Gifts, or Quarto Kids.

This edition published in 2022 by Wellfleet Press, an imprint of The Quarto Group, 142 West 36th Street, 4th Floor, New York, NY 10018, USA
T (212) 779-4972 F (212) 779-6058 www.QuartoKnows.com

Contains content previously published in expanded format in 2020 by Wellfleet Press, an imprint of The Quarto Group, 142 West 36th Street, 4th Floor, New York, NY 10018, USA.

Wellfleet titles are also available at discount for retail, wholesale, promotional, and bulk purchase. For details, contact the Special Sales Manager by email at specialsales@quarto.com or by mail at The Quarto Group, Attn: Special Sales Manager, 100 Cummings Center Suite 265D, Beverly, MA 01915 USA.

10 9 8 7 6 5 4 3 2 1

ISBN: 978-1-57715-316-0

Publisher: Rage Kindelsperger | Creative Director: Laura Drew | Managing Editor: Cara Donaldson
Senior Editor: John Foster | Cover Design: Andrea Ho | Interior Design: Kate Smith |
Illustrations by Sosha Davis with the exception of pages 24, 36, 73, 91, and 122 © Shutterstock

Printed in Singapore

This book provides general information on various widely known and widely accepted theories on sleep and dream interpretation. However, it should not be relied upon as recommending or promoting any specific diagnosis or method of treatment for a particular condition, and it is not intended as a substitute for medical advice or for direct diagnosis and treatment of a medical condition by a qualified physician. Readers who have questions about a particular condition, possible treatments for that condition, or possible reactions from the condition or its treatment should consult a physician or other qualified health-care professional.